NO-LOAD
DIVORCE

HOW TO SAVE MONEY, TIME, AND SELF-RESPECT AS YOU END YOUR MARRIAGE

Bill Kumm & Steve Case

Financial Independence, Inc.

No-Load Divorce
How to Save Money, Time, and Self-Respect as You End Your Marriage
By Bill Kumm and Steve Case

Published by Financial Independence Publications
3883 Telegraph Road, Suite 204
Bloomfield Hills, Michigan 48302
Phone: (248) 644-7080 Fax: (248) 644-6145
www.noloaddivorce.com

This publication contains the opinions and ideas of its authors. It is designed to provide accurate and authoritative information in regard to the subject matter covered. It is sold with the understanding that the publisher is not engaged in rendering professional services. If legal, accounting, financial, medical, psychological or any other expert assistance is required, the services of a competent professional person should be sought. The authors and publisher specifically disclaim any responsibility for any liability, loss or risk, personal or otherwise, which is incurred as a consequence, directly or indirectly, of the use and application of any of the contents of this book. All material in this book is original except where attributed. Stories are of actual people, but their names and circumstances have been changed to provide them with privacy where requested. Any similarity with existing published information is coincidental and accidental.

ISBN 0-9723630-0-9

Visit www.noloaddivorce.com
Printed in the United States of America

Cover photo by Leftheris Papageorgiou of Hellenic Adventures, Minneapolis
Cover design by Kyle G. Hunter
Book design by Wendy Holdman
Typesetting by Stanton Publication Services, Inc., St. Paul

Contents

Acknowledgments

›› Bill Kumm

To my children, Lauren and Billy, who showed maturity beyond their years during the divorce of their parents. I'm proud of you.

To Malissa Loutzenhiser, my assistant, who has helped immeasurably in managing my time split between business, children, and the writing of this book. I'm grateful to you.

To my mother, Alice Marron, who raised five children without child support or alimony, yet never said a negative word about the husband who abandoned her. I love you, Mom.

And to my father, Dan Marron, who stepped in and raised me and my four siblings after my biological father left when I was six years old. Thank you for introducing me to the outdoors.

›› Steve Case

To my three girls, Isabella, Alexandra, and Victoria, who inspire me daily. And to my wife, Cheryl Case, for your support, insights, sense of humor (she wondered what was behind my decision to become a Certified Divorce Planner), and for your commitment to our strong marriage.

The authors would also like to thank the clergy, mediators, lawyers, counselors, and other divorce professionals who contributed to this book. We mention many of you, but we want you all to know how much we appreciate your wise counsel. And we extend our sincere thanks to the scores of people who shared their divorce stories with us. Without your bravery, the book would not be as good.

Finally, a special thanks to our editorial advisers, Gary Legwold and Rick Naymark, who helped us convert ideas and sentences into a book. Our gratitude also goes to Kathy Weflen and Mary Keirstead, who edited the book.

Introduction

Financial planners Bill Kumm and Steve Case never intended to write a book on divorce. Their lives were full enough, running their Detroit-area business and being involved with their families. Then, in 1997, Bill went through a divorce—a nasty, expensive divorce that drained his bank account of $25,000.

It was tough enough for Bill to spend that kind of money to end the marriage he had such high hopes for, but it was even tougher to discover later that he could have spent far less. Bill made the classic mistake of doing what he assumed everyone did: he immediately turned his divorce over to a lawyer. But his lawyer led to another lawyer, for Bill's spouse, and the two lawyers went at it, quickly establishing an adversarial situation.

Bill's lawyer did not inform Bill that he could do much of the paperwork himself. Nor did the lawyer tell him that many of the decisions involved with divorce are cut and dried. That is, many decisions are settled according to state or local guidelines or in accordance with what the courts traditionally consider fair.

After the divorce was finalized and the huge legal bill had been paid, Bill realized his divorce—indeed, most divorces—needn't be costly or contentious. He looked back at the process and was disgusted at the expensive legal dead ends into which he had been led. Bill was furious at a divorce system loaded with legal and emotional costs.

Not only was Bill upset about how much money he spent on his case, but he also fumed as he thought about the countless other couples paying for needlessly expensive divorces.

Someone, Bill thought, must tell people that divorce needn't be so loaded with legal and emotional costs. Yes, every divorce will have legal fees, and certainly divorces are painful. But Bill wanted to tell people that they have the means to limit legal bills and the personal pain of divorce.

Indeed, if people were to learn—*before* and *while* they were going through the divorce process, not *afterward*—about the financial realities of divorce in a straightforward fashion, then they could more readily choose to compromise, cooperate, and keep their self-respect as they divorce. The result would be a less expensive, less burdensome divorce—a "no-load" divorce.

Divorce and Crucial Decisions about Finances

As Bill was going through his travails, Steve—who is not divorced—initially saw his role as being a supportive friend and business partner. However, as Steve listened to Bill's accounts, he began to realize that Bill's complaints were similar to the complaints of many of Steve's clients who were also going through a divorce. The clients were making the same mistakes Bill had made, which meant they were wasting money.

Financial planners don't like to see their clients waste money. So Steve felt compelled to advise his clients that there is a way of going through a divorce that is less loaded with legal and emotional costs than the prevailing system.

Not only did Bill and Steve believe they could help people save money during their divorce, but they also appreciated in a new way just what a financially crucial time a couple confronts when a marriage ends. They also firmly believed that with some simple, timely advice about insurance, estate planning, and investments, divorcing couples could make wise decisions about their financial future.

With their future already jumbled, the last thing divorcing people want is to have their finances jumbled as well. Each spouse wants a solid financial plan that factors in the realities of life after divorce.

When Bill's divorce was over, Bill and Steve began talking about writing a book on divorce and finances. Their "no-load" divorce advice to their divorcing clients was proving to be invaluable, and they felt they couldn't just sit on this concept while thousands of people were paying too much for their divorces and then floundering financially.

The Birth of No-Load Divorce

Finally, about a year ago, Bill and Steve agreed that they must write this book. The decision was made as Bill continued to experience the consequences of his bad divorce, long after the divorce had been finalized. Bill wanted to explain to readers what he knew firsthand, namely, to take care in making decisions during a divorce because they will affect you for years. With regret, he saw that his life today would have been better had he experienced a "no-load" divorce.

Bill still had ongoing conflicts with his ex-wife—and a few times with her second husband. Bill spent another $20,000 in legal fees on an attempted change in custody. There have been and are hassles about changing schools and taking vacations with the kids. His relationship with his children is changing, sometimes in ways that make him sad and uncomfortable. The ramifications of this divorce continue.

A book was a natural vehicle to explain the concept of "no-load' divorce, but Bill and Steve still had one reservation about the book. They wondered if people, so used to turning divorce matters over to an attorney, could handle this kind of "do-it-yourself" divorce. Would people be intimidated by the process?

They asked a panel of professionals specializing in divorce (lawyers, psychologists, clergy, mediators, and social workers) to evaluate their concept. The panel agreed that, with the proper basic instruction, many divorcing couples could successfully navigate a "no-load" divorce. This was both exciting and encouraging to Bill and Steve. So, drawing on the many hours of discussions with these professionals and on their experiences helping divorcing couples untangle their finances, they gathered their best advice into a book describing the "no-load" divorce process.

This, then, is the birth of the No-Load Divorce, a better way to experience a divorce. In writing this book, Bill and Steve have prepared an easy-to-follow guide about divorce. They want you to be knowledgeable so that you can be respectful and savvy during the divorce and upbeat about your future after the divorce.

Before moving into chapter 1, a few notes about the book. First, starting in chapter 1, the authors write in the first-person plural voice. Therefore, when you read "we," you know that both Bill and Steve are writing to you. There are occasions when Bill or Steve will speak singularly, but the book is a team effort.

Second, the authors use the terms *lawyer* and *attorney* interchangeably. Finally, this book is meant for any couple going through a divorce. Although the authors discuss many issues specific to couples with children, they realize that childless couples also experience pain during a divorce and need financial guidance as well.

The Editors

CHAPTER 1

Don't Make Divorce Tougher Than It Is

Going through a divorce can can be the most traumatic experience in a lifetime. It deeply affects you, your spouse, children, extended family, and friends. The painful process of ending a marriage that you once had so many hopes for will bring with it several "loads"—financial, emotional, physical, and spiritual—that will weigh on you the rest of your life.

A divorce is full of feelings and decisions. Unfortunately, the two don't mix well. Anger, to name one predominant emotion during a divorce, can cloud your decision making and lead to a costly, knock-down-drag-out divorce in which all of the loads of divorce become needlessly magnified. In the process, you, your children—and your finances—are burdened even more.

This can be avoided. You can have an ugly divorce fully loaded with bitterness and legal fees, or you can *decide* to lighten your loads and have a No-Load Divorce.

›› What Is a No-Load Divorce?

Simply put, a No-Load Divorce minimizes the loads—especially the costs. You lessen the financial and emotional loads. If you have children, a No-Load Divorce helps you avoid custody battles, which incur front- and back-end charges on the happiness of you and your children.

In a No-Load Divorce, you take control of the process, but at the same time you are supported by a team of professionals—not just one lawyer. Advising you will be a family counselor/therapist, mediator, and financial adviser. A lawyer has a limited but important role in the divorce. This team will guide you through a very defined process and will encourage collaboration and cooperation with your spouse as you work toward agreements. We'll explain the process in greater detail later.

We are excited about the concept and benefits of the No-Load Divorce, and we have asked for feedback from other professionals. We sought out lawyers to understand if there could be a less costly and less contentious way to solve divorce issues so that couples could avoid the average $15,000 cost of a divorce in the United States and spend about one-fifth of that for a No-Load Divorce. We spoke with child psychologists, marriage counselors, mediators, and court-appointed negotiators. All seemed to echo our enthusiasm. In all their years of advising clients, they said they had seen too many needlessly knotty and badly botched divorces to not appreciate our concept. They said the No-Load Divorce rang true to them.

›› Is the No-Load Divorce for You?

The No-Load Divorce is a blessing for many people going through a divorce, but, unfortunately, it is not for every couple.

We recently had a couple in our office who illustrated the type of people this book does *not* target. As we began to inventory their assets as a means of establishing a baseline for property settlement, the husband stood up and excused himself to go to the restroom. While he was out of the room, his wife leaned forward and whispered, "For years he's been hiding money. I'm almost positive he's got a girlfriend. He gives her $10,000 each year, and $10,000 to each of her three children. He's been doing this for five years. How can I get my share of that $200,000?"

The husband returned from the restroom, and shortly thereafter the wife excused herself to use the restroom. While she was gone, the husband leaned forward and whispered, "I think there's something you should know. She's got a boyfriend. I'm almost sure of it. He sends her beautiful diamond jewelry. I've seen it hidden in her dresser drawers in the bedroom. How do I get half the value of that?"

We knew we couldn't work with the couple on fair asset distribution. We knew they were not candidates for a No-Load Divorce. As David L. Harrison, JD, a divorce attorney in Rochester, Michigan, says, "No-Load Divorce is only as good as the parties are honest. The couple needs traditional legal help when one or both of them hide assets, transfer money into other accounts, or otherwise squirrel money away."

That is one example of the types of couples and individuals this book is *not* for. In addition, this book is not for:

The threatening spouse

This is the spouse who may feel helpless but masks that feeling of inadequacy in threats. His or her approach to negotiations starts with something like, "I'm leaving the state, I'm taking our children with me, and you'll never see them again." Or, "You can rot in poverty, because I'm not giving you one red cent." These threats are not discussion starters. Usually, they are quick, one-way tickets to high-powered and expensive attorneys.

Harrison had one such client. He was her fifth attorney in efforts to stop her ex-husband from seeing their child. The father was fighting to change the custody agreement because the mother had nearly 100 percent custody. She claimed he was a poor father because the father would do things like fail to return the child's lunch box when the father brought the boy home.

"The court ruled that the mom simply was no longer acting in the child's best interest," says Harrison. "Because of her insistence on fighting about almost everything—her obsession with the battle, the righteous fight—she lost almost all custody. And her total legal bill was well over $100,000. My share alone was between $6,000 and $7,000. I finally filed a motion to withdraw from the case."

Couples with a serious dysfunction

The process is not appropriate in situations where there is spousal physical abuse, child abuse, or child neglect. In these cases, there are legitimate reasons to use the courts and lawyers to protect all parties and to seek a fair solution that could not be negotiated by the couple alone.

Game players

Some people say they want a divorce, but they really don't. They want to stay married and be in a continuous state of getting a divorce because that is an effective way of engaging their spouse's attention. Game players play loose with the truth, like to blame, and don't like closure. Their favorite phrase is, "Yes, but . . ."

Game players often put their children through cruel loyalty tests. For example, Harrison says one of his clients had a son who was a good athlete. The father's custody time was severely limited. He did not have custody when the boy played in baseball games. Nevertheless, he attended the games.

"The mom would chastise the boy for looking at the father first when the boy did something well," says Harrison. "She'd say to the boy, 'After you hit that home run, why did you look at your dad and not me first?' And then she'd litigate to limit the father's parenting time even more. She'd discharge lawyers who counseled peace and seek lawyers who said they would support her desire for war."

Emotional wrecks

Let's face it, if you can't get a handle on your emotions, you can't be a candidate for No-Load Divorce. Understandably, high emotions are part of the divorce process. But you must distance your emotions from the practical side of the process. Emotions counter logic, collaboration, and reason, all of which are necessary for the No-Load Divorce.

We once had a client who was understandably attached to her house and would not think of giving it up during her divorce proceedings. She fought for the house and won. The house turned out to be what we call an "alligator" because it ate a lot of cash as the client made payments and did maintenance. Finally, it ate all her cash, and she was forced to sell. She would have been better off putting her emotions aside, parting with the house, and taking other assets as part of the settlement.

So, now you have a pretty good idea who will not succeed at No-Load Divorce. But what kind of people will be successful? Perhaps this is best answered by one of our professional advisers, Lynn Lott, a marriage and family therapist from Richmond, California:

"I tell my clients there is a hard way and an easy way to get a divorce. The hard way is to go though a battle using lawyers. The easy way is what I would call the nonadversarial divorce, or the No-Load Divorce. Couples have to say, 'We don't want to be married. We're not going to get back together. We don't want to be disrespectful. We know each of us will feel loss, but what can we do so this is not a bloodbath?'"

Lott says, "The number of couples who are willing to follow the No-Load Divorce is growing. More and more people I see want to go through a nonadversarial divorce. They may be using attorneys, but they are using a marriage counselor too, and they are in control of the process."

Lott's last point, about control, is important in defining whom this book is for. *The book is for divorcing people who want to be in control of their divorce and who also put a premium on cooperation.* You begin losing control when you turn over too much of your divorce to lawyers, who may advise not talking to your spouse.

To get to this point of control and cooperation, you may need a cooling-off period, when you work through a variety of strong emotions using a family counselor, marriage therapist, your clergy, or all of the above. Sometimes couples need time apart. It also helps to have worked out some of the many details around property and children, so that you have evidence of your ability to compromise and be fair to each other.

At the end of the day, though, you want to be in control of the process. Because divorce occurs at a time of vulnerability, high emotions, and stress, the temptation is to look for someone to handle the divorce for you, like a lawyer. But delegating can set up immediate defensiveness in the mind of your spouse, who then may react by turning everything over to his or her lawyer. Then, two lawyers begin to work out your divorce issues instead of you. You have begun to lose control and communication with your spouse.

Sometimes, a lawyer-directed divorce can be done respectfully and cost-effectively. Other times, however, lawyers, who are trained in adversarial problem solving, tend to increase the hostility. Lawyers, too, must act in ways that protect their practice liability, making sure they represent your interests to the highest degree. In many instances, this stance leaves little room for trust and collaboration. A battle begins. Legal fees can skyrocket. The process drags on. All participants get more emotionally hurt. However, you and your divorcing spouse can control the process. You can set the ground rules, determine the agenda, agree on the issues, and seek out a fair solution. You can direct your mediator, your lawyers, and the court to pay attention to your wishes. In this scenario, resolution is more likely, with less cost, time, and emotional strain.

So, if you want to control the process of your divorce and cooperate to achieve the ending most desirable for you, your spouse, and your children, this book will show you how.

›› Four Fundamental Reasons No-Load Divorce Works

1. Divorce need not be contentious.

All too often, divorce is set up as an adversarial process. "Get a lawyer" is often the first advice the husband and wife hear. Hiring lawyers, however, immediately sets up an adversarial relationship. Usually the immediate legal advice is, "Don't discuss anything with your spouse. Let the lawyers talk to each other on your behalf." We disagree with this advice. Using this approach, how can couples discuss issues and begin negotiations?

The divorce process needn't start out that way. Doug, a friend of ours, went through his divorce smoothly. Both he and his wife were committed to rising above the tempting, dispute-everything fray that is almost a cliché in divorce. They wanted to work out a settlement that would benefit them all, especially their two children. They were determined to do it the No-Load Divorce way and not make a tough situation worse.

Steve has a friend who went to an attorney for help in ending a one-and-a-half-year marriage. The attorney, unfortunately, urged him to do battle. Steve advised his friend to avoid getting sucked into the emotional black holes of divorce. Steve urged him, instead, to do what was necessary to get the divorce done and to not get into arguments. There will be problems in any divorce, but you don't necessarily have to use lawyers to address emotional hurt. That strategy could result in what amounts to counseling sessions in front of an expensive non-counselor—a $300-per-hour attorney.

Harrison says lawyers spend many billable hours dealing with emotional issues for which they have no formal training. "And yet these issues are at least as important—or more important—to the case as the legal issues," he says. "Often, I will spend more of my time trying to channel my client's frustrations and anger toward a peaceful resolution than I do on the phone discussing the legal aspects of the case with the opposing lawyer. And clients get billed the same rate whether I am being a divorce attorney or a person providing emotional support."

A couple of qualifiers are in order: First, we are not into lawyer bashing. Attorneys play a limited but important role in No-Load Divorce, which we will explain throughout the book. Second, the No-Load Divorce approach will not fit every couple and every circumstance. Couples in some complex cases, involving splitting businesses, for example, may need complex legal help during the divorce process. We will explain more about these exceptions in subsequent chapters.

The important point here is this: Divorce settlements, no matter how complex or how involved attorneys are, need not be contentious.

2. Divorce need not be costly.

Divorce courts in most states follow similar rules about what they consider to be a fair and acceptable dissolution. It's like our friend Doug says: "About 90 percent of divorce decisions are not really decisions. They are rules and guidelines set up by the state."

So Doug did much of his divorce work himself, the No-Load Divorce way. "And I'm not a do-it-yourselfer. I don't change my own oil or fix my own toilet or anything," he says. "Divorce does not have to be complex. With many issues, there is just not much legal wiggle room."

Lawyers can contribute to the complexity of a divorce. If lawyers stir up emotions, they may create more suspicion and more battles between the divorcing people, thus prolonging the legal process and increasing the cost. If, on the other hand, lawyers encourage movement toward generally acceptable guidelines about division of property and child custody, they can help shorten the process and keep legal costs reasonable.

What a divorce lawyer may not tell you is this: It is possible for a lawyer, in only half an hour or so, to lay out settlement guidelines and a fairly accurate picture of what your settlement will be. As Doug said, about 90 percent of the rules and guidelines are set up by the state. You can go to our Web site, www.noloaddivorce.com, for settlement guideline information by state for cases that do not have extenuating circumstances. Divorcing couples can use these guidelines as a starting point in their negotiations, knowing that divorce courts generally consider them to be fair.

Keeping legal costs reasonable is within the control of people seeking a divorce. Attorney Harrison explains that emotional turmoil is costly to divorcing people, and that many lawyers make every effort to reduce the emotional turmoil and reach a fair settlement.

"But Lord knows there are plenty of lawyers whose goal is not to help their client get through the divorce with the least amount of conflict," he says. "They can set the stage to decrease trust and communications between the parties. They take on the worst qualities of their client, and they like to 'stay in the flames,' making a bad situation worse. There is no doubt that you can bill more hours in a bloody battle than in a peaceful resolution, but I should say this is not a universal component of most lawyers."

Harrison is quick to add that for every lawyer who likes to put gas on the fire, "there is certainly a client who is bitter and wants to keep the battle going too. We try to help these people, but they cannot see past their own self-interest. They cannot help themselves, or they lack the capacity—because of depression or alcoholism, for example—to approach the situation in any reasonable manner. You give them advice and they nod their head, but then they seize on an issue in order to vent at their spouse."

3. Results will usually be similar no matter which process couples follow.

In most cases, our professional panel said that their experience seems to support the theory that justice is blind and fair, and leans toward the typical guidelines. This is true if the parties have a long and bitter fight. This is true if they get down to business fast and get the divorce over with. What we are saying is the end point is more or less the same either way, but the cost will definitely be different. We like to think of the difference in these terms: With the get-down-to-business route, the $10,000 to $25,000 you save on legal costs could send your child to a top college for a year or even fund a complete college education, depending on the child's age at the time of the divorce and how the money grows over time. With the long-and-bitter-fight route, your money goes to lawyers. As a result, a friend of ours quipped, your child goes to a community college while your attorney's child goes to Harvard!

›› WHAT YOUR DIVORCE MONEY COULD BE DOING!

If you had a contentious divorce 16 years ago and paid $30,000 in legal fees, you didn't spend just $30,000. You spent the investment potential of that money as well. Had you been able to save a net of $25,000 in legal fees by having a No-Load Divorce and invested it, you would have substantially more money today that could help your children attend college or contribute to a more secure retirement.

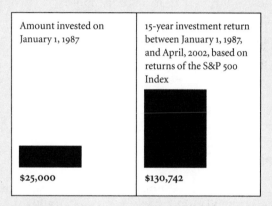

Amount invested on January 1, 1987	15-year investment return between January 1, 1987, and April, 2002, based on returns of the S&P 500 Index
$25,000	$130,742

Here is a scenario of how an investment of $25,000 over the 15-year period of 1987–2002 (April) could have performed. All figures are before tax, with reinvested dividends. Source: Morningstar.

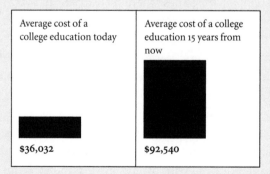

Average cost of a college education today	Average cost of a college education 15 years from now
$36,032	$92,540

Four years of in-state tuition, fees, room and board at a public four-year college, based on 2001–2002 school year. Source: The College Board, "Trends in College Pricing," 2001.

4. The biggest problem with divorcing couples is lack of knowledge of the legal system.

Naturally, most couples don't understand the legal process and the court system, and they don't know the guidelines for property settlements, legal and physical custody of children, alimony, and child support.

Bill paid dearly for his lack of knowledge about divorce. He and his wife wanted a divorce, and the lawyers dragged the process out for six months, which cost Bill $25,000. Bill had put his trust in his lawyer, who hadn't informed Bill that mediation could be used in the divorce process. Bill learned about mediation himself and asked his lawyer why he and his wife were not mediating. The lawyer's response was, "Oh, is that what you wanted?"

Bill's case was then mediated and settled on state guidelines for splitting of assets, child support, alimony, and so on. The bottom line is the divorce could have been done in much less time for far less money.

›› A Typical Divorce Process

How is a divorce usually accomplished? In most cases, one person initiates the divorce. That person hires a lawyer and files for divorce. Then the other spouse hires a lawyer. Since most states have no-fault divorce laws where there is no requirement to prove that one spouse caused the divorce to happen, the issues that must be resolved concern property settlements, custody of the children, alimony, and child support. One spouse usually moves out of the house.

Next is the "discovery" period, when the lawyers seek full and honest inventories of property as well as information for structuring the child custody. Each spouse asks questions of the other through the lawyers in a formal, written manner, called *interrogatories*. This discovery period may take months and is costly. Usually, each spouse explains why he or she needs more property and why the other spouse would not be a good parent. Trust goes out the window. An adversarial atmosphere intensifies. Often, agreement on even the smallest points seems impossible.

After about six months (but it could go longer), the spouses' anger has developed into hate for each other. The children are confused and distraught, and the attorneys start to look for common ground. About this time, the attorneys tell them what they should have told them at the start—that there are generally accepted guidelines for settlement.

The attorneys trade draft agreements back and forth. Little progress is made, and the case is then mediated. The mediator is usually another attorney, which means more costs because the couple is now paying three attorneys. Finally, both spouses are exhausted, stressed, bitter, and frustrated by the mounting costs. Their physical and emotional health—and their children's physical and emotional health—has probably worsened. So they reluctantly agree on a settlement. Then the settlement is drawn up and presented to the court (more legal costs). One or both parties appear with the lawyer(s) in court, and the divorce is approved.

Neither party thinks the deal is fair. They are left with large legal bills, as well as the expense of supporting two households and the challenge of co-parenting with the person they have argued with for at least a year.

›› The No-Load Divorce Process

The No-Load Divorce process has 10 steps. All steps are necessary, and you should follow them in order. We summarize the steps here and explain them in greater detail as we move through the remainder of the book.

Here are the essential details of each step.

STEP 1:
Make sure the marriage is over, and commit to the No-Load Divorce process.

When you marry, the typical vow is "for better or for worse, till death do us part." Unfortunately, for many people the vow boils down to "for better, or until I become unhappy or sick of this person."

We understand that divorce is best for many marriages. However, too many divorces happen for reasons that don't warrant such drastic action. For example, if people are unhappy with themselves, sometimes they look to others, like a spouse, to blame for their discontent. Don't be blinded by your discontent. Happiness is an inside job, and too many people who get a divorce are trying to find happiness "outside," in other people and situations.

You must do everything in your power to make sure your marriage is over before you commit to the divorce process. The last thing you need is to finally get your divorce and then wonder: "Is this what I really wanted?"

We have a friend whose marriage to a beautiful but fanciful woman started to crumble. Together they had a son, whom they both loved. The friend was a scientist, and his wife was an art teacher at a local community college. At first, their different orientations to life drew them together. However, over time they realized that their basic differences made it difficult for them to be compatible.

As our friend contemplated his divorce, he was in agony. "The idea of being a failure seemed unforgivable to me," he told us. "I can't leave this marriage. I have to find a way to make it work."

We observed our friend as he went through three years of painful marriage counseling, with his wife and alone. He seemed to need to talk about the process for hours on end. As time went on, it was hard for us to be patient with him, for we saw the inevitable. Finally, one day at lunch, we asked him why he seemed to be prolonging the breakup.

"I have to make sure it's over," he said. "I want to leave this marriage without a shadow of a doubt. Then, and only then, will I feel good about myself and be ready to move on with my life."

Our friend's experience should be a lesson to you if you are contemplating divorce—especially if you have children.

Once you agree the marriage is over, you must now commit to the process of No-Load Divorce with your spouse. It takes two to successfully complete the No-Load Divorce. The No-Load Divorce is not a unilateral decision. You cannot have one person acting rationally and in the interest of collaboration and fairness while the other person is raging, throwing temper tantrums, and secretly meeting with a lawyer to plot strategy.

In addition to a commitment to the process, both of you must agree to open and frequent communication. The No-Load Divorce process requires back-and-forth, give-and-take work that cannot be done strictly by letter. In Doug's case, he made a mistake in the divorce settlement regarding custody. He and his ex-wife revisited the issue after papers were signed, and she agreed to change the wording. No bickering, no fuss. The change just made sense for all parties involved. This is an example of how the No-Load Divorce can work. But if each party is documenting everything and looking for ways to trip up the other, the process will deteriorate. If you want a contentious divorce—which is your choice—No-Load Divorce is not for you.

The last part of this committing-to-the-process step is about closure. In most dysfunctional marriages, arguments are never resolved. Grudges continue. You never quite get through and over disagreements. Perhaps the reason Doug was so committed to seeing the No-Load Divorce through to the end was that his parents were just the opposite during their divorce. "They fought over things like blenders," he says. "For four years, they had a drag-out-everything, hate-filled, nuclear, no-one-wins battle. They would spend $2,000 on something as silly as making sure the other person would not get the lawn mower. I learned that you couldn't want to win the battle. You have to be able to compromise.

"I lived in the battle for 30 years. It was always there. At my wedding, I

›› HOW CAN WE COMMUNICATE *NOW* WHEN WE COULDN'T BEFORE?

It would be fair for you to raise the obvious objection: "If my spouse and I had been able to have frequent and open communication and agree to follow the same process, we wouldn't necessarily have to be divorced. So isn't this contradictory? We're getting a divorce because we can't work together."

There is more to a marriage than the ability to work together, and there is more to a divorce than the inability to work together. You can go round and round on this, but the bottom line is you need to work together in the No-Load Divorce process because it is in the best interest of you and your children. Your marriage may be dissolved, but for years to come, you will need to negotiate hundreds of details and issues involved with joint parenting. You could look at the process of No-Load Divorce as the start of finding a new way to communicate that is less emotional and less tied to your marriage history. This is more about your new relationship as two separate people. Part of the success of this new relationship, then, is an agreement that you are both willing to learn how to communicate with honesty and frequency.

had to worry about having Mom and Dad in the same room. Parents' Day at college, graduations, birthdays—they were all positive events that became negative because my parents kept living in the battle."

This living in the battle has to change for you to be successful at No-Load Divorce. A No-Load Divorce has an end point. You reach an agreement. It is drawn up and included in the divorce order, and the divorce is over. We cannot emphasize enough that at the start of the No-Load Divorce process, both of you need to agree on a commitment to closure in a reasonable amount of time.

STEP 2:
Learn about divorce issues with the help of our Starting Point plan (on www.noloaddivorce.com).

Once you are certain the marriage is over, you need some understanding of the divorce issues that lie ahead. When most divorcing people come to us, they are just beginning to split up. Their emotions are raw, and the tension in the room is palpable. They are hurt, confused, and overwhelmed about the magnitude of this event. What they don't know is there are generally accepted rules about nearly everything involved in divorce—custody, visitation, alimony, child support, and the division of property. The judges know these rules and adhere to them within reason. In other words, a judge won't accept a settlement that seems to be too far outside the bounds of these accepted rules.

For this reason you need to learn how these divorce rules apply to your particular situation. To help you learn, we've developed what we call the Starting Point plan, which you'll find on our Web site. The plan asks you for data about your financial and divorce situation. Once you input the data, the program prepares a likely divorce settlement. This gives you an idea what the divorce court defines as a generally acceptable agreement.

Starting Point will help you split assets and make two important calculations. The first is an estimated alimony payment. The second is an estimated child support payment. Since each state's or county's alimony and child support formulas and calculations may be different, determining these two amounts would be difficult without legal help—but easy if you use Starting Point.

Starting Point also addresses:

▸ The standards for splitting the assets based on factors such as current income needs, children's college education, retirement planning, and purchase of a new home.

▸ Insurance needs. This includes individual insurance to cover alimony and child support obligations in case of death or disability.

STEP 3:

Meet separately with your financial adviser to begin discussions about your individual financial plan.

In all cases, and especially in cases involving children and significant assets, we recommend financial planning assistance. There are many long-lasting decisions involving financial matters during a divorce. We recommend that you use financial advisers affiliated with the No-Load Divorce network. You can locate them on our Web site. These financial advisers are trained in the No-Load Divorce process and are committed to it. Your financial adviser should be licensed and have the proper qualifications to enact the transactions you will need. Financial advisers affiliated with the No-Load Divorce process have the expertise or arrangements with other professionals to cover alimony calculations, child support calculations, business valuations, pension division, and tax implications. They can help you project your financial future based on the outcome of the divorce.

STEP 4:

Separately begin the No-Load Divorce worksheet

The complete No-Load Divorce worksheet is in chapter 7. If you completed the Starting Point plan, you can transfer the information to the worksheet. The worksheet addresses the areas and issues you must consider and negotiate in formulating your No-Load Divorce agreement. You can make copies of this worksheet or download it from our Web site and then start filling in the blanks.

STEP 5:

*Hold your first session together with your No-Load Divorce mediator
to discuss the ground rules and process for negotiation.*

To experience a No-Load Divorce, you and your spouse must agree to select one No-Load Divorce mediator whom you will pay to be impartial
and represent both of your interests. In chapter 4, we'll offer resources
and suggestions for finding the right mediator for your situation. A No-
Load Divorce mediator allows each of you to have a say in what would be
a fair settlement. You can meet face-to-face, hear each other firsthand,
and avoid the possible third-party innuendos that can occur by speaking
through lawyers.

Agreeing on a No-Load Divorce mediator up front is a key differentia-
tion in the No-Load Divorce process. Most divorcing couples do not
take this step. Usually, they select lawyers and start battling. If they have
children and cannot agree on a custody arrangement, the court often as-
signs a family evaluation to be done by a court-appointed professional.
No matter what the lawyers say, the judge often adopts the evaluator's ultimate suggestions as to how the custody should be arranged.

Most couples think their lawyers can heavily influence the custody
arrangement. Then they start building a case for how the other spouse is
an incompetent parent. In most cases, though, the spouse is not an incompetent parent; the spouses are just different parents.

However, if you have concerns of possible child abuse or endangerment, or fears that the other spouse will leave town with the children,
then you do need to take legal action to protect your rights and to protect
the children. No-Load Divorce is not for couples facing these situations.

We are suggesting that you follow three steps in trying to work out
custody issues:

1. Try to work out a custody arrangement with your spouse.

2. If you need help, try to work out an agreement together with
   your No-Load Divorce mediator.

3. If you cannot reach an agreement, ask for a court-appointed
   evaluator to help you determine the custody arrangement.

If there are issues of child endangerment or abuse, you should consult with your attorney.

STEP 6:

Together, meet and negotiate items on the No-Load Divorce worksheet. Return together to the mediator and resolve outstanding issues until the worksheet is completed.

When you and your spouse have completed the worksheet, or at least as much as you can agree on, you will use it as the basis for your proposed agreement. The worksheet specifies the mediated settlement you and your spouse deem equitable and appropriate to your circumstances. It addresses the essential elements of property division; spousal maintenance (sometimes called alimony or transition payments); legal and physical custody of the children; the custody schedule; and how to handle retirement plans, trusts, and other financial instruments with long-term consequences.

This agreement represents the culmination of your collaboration to develop a fair and equitable settlement that is under your control and that has been completed with respect for each party. You can change the agreement at any time before your final settlement is filed with the court. But if you followed the No-Load Divorce process, you will probably require only minor legal revisions going forward.

Undoubtedly, there will be areas with which you need the help of your No-Load Divorce mediator to reach understanding and consensus. Your mediator will help you make the progress necessary to reach an final proposed agreement pending legal review.

STEP 7:

Meet with your financial adviser to review the proposed agreement and its impact on your financial plan.

The adviser reviews the suggested division of assets, alimony, and child support and provides you with a cash-flow analysis. The adviser also looks at tax liabilities of various potential outcomes and reviews pension disposition. Based on your proposed agreement, the adviser can prepare a financial profile to answer questions such as: When can I retire? How much do I need to save for retirement or college for my children? How will my financial picture look in 5 to 10 years?

STEP 8:
Review the proposed agreement with your No-Load Divorce lawyer and discuss issues to be changed.

While legal representation may not be required in all states, we have made it a part of the No-Load Divorce process. We believe that a legal review can uncover potential problems that were unintended by either party. This review can lead to amendments to the agreement, prior to submission to the divorce court.

We recommend that *each* spouse retain separate legal representation. This creates a balance of power and a "fail-safe" method to make sure that your agreement is fair.

As part of the No-Load Divorce process, we recommend that you retain No-Load Divorce lawyers. We list them on our Web site. To qualify for listing, these lawyers agree to operate according to our No-Load Divorce principles. They must have knowledge of divorce law and an orientation toward fairness and finality. They must agree to follow the No-Load Divorce process and use the No-Load Divorce agreement.

It would not serve the process for you to hire lawyers bent on conflict, delay, and "winning." All this would do is reopen emotional wounds and boost the legal costs. If you want that type of legal representation, you should not begin the No-Load Divorce process.

Keep in mind that the two-lawyer review is built into the No-Load Divorce process from the start. That way, both you and your spouse will be inclined to be fair as you go through the first five steps, primarily relying on a mediator but knowing that legal review will occur. If changes have been made to the agreement, you should review them again with your financial adviser.

STEP 9:
Have one lawyer draft a final agreement and file it with the court as part of a petition for divorce.

Once your financial adviser assures you that the agreement is reasonable, or at least in line with previous discussions, the next step is for one of your lawyers, usually the lawyer of the spouse who originally filed for divorce, to draw up the final agreement. The final agreement will be incorporated into a formal settlement and petition for divorce, and filed with the court. When it is submitted to the court, the court will set a date for a hearing. The judge (or a referee representing the judge) will accept the petition and issue a decree granting the divorce.

STEP 10:

Work with your financial adviser to re-title assets according to the agreement and enact the financial plan, which should include updated individual estate plans.

Once the divorce is final, your new life is just beginning. You need to implement all the parts of your agreement. Your financial adviser will help you re-title the assets that are yours (including pensions or other retirement plans), change beneficiaries, make sure you have the necessary insurance, invest assets according to your financial plan, address estate planning needs, and take care of other relevant financial issues.

We don't wish a divorce on anybody, and we urge you to carefully read the next chapter, "Are You Sure It's Over? If It Is . . ." Our hope is that after you read this chapter, you won't read any further because you won't need a divorce. However, the sad fact is many of you will need a divorce, which is tough emotionally and financially. We know this from our own experience and from the experiences of our clients. Don't make divorce any tougher than it is. Make this a No-Load Divorce.

CHAPTER 2

Are You Sure It's Over? If It Is . . .

Frank looks back at his life 25 years ago. He shakes his head at what might have been. He had been married three years, and he and his wife, Donna, had two young children. He was a real estate agent, and his houses weren't moving. Money was tight. Frank didn't spend much time with his family because he worked long hours, even on Sundays. He was a deacon at his church, but he quit attending because he was showing houses.

Frank and Donna slowly grew apart. She started working to help make ends meet. They began developing separate interests. One of Frank's interests was another woman. "I became numb to God and my family," he says. "But it was nice to have someone notice me, in a physical way, even though I knew my heart was at home."

At home, Frank and Donna went through a period of saying "Hi" and "Bye" and not much in between. They had major arguments, but as they grew further and further apart, the arguments were fewer and fewer. "We were going nowhere fast," Frank says.

Donna found out about Frank's affair, and she received all sorts of advice to divorce him. But one friend gave her different advice: Pray for Frank and continue to love him.

"Donna called me at my girlfriend's house," Frank recalls. "She said, 'I know where you are and who you are with, Frank, but I love you and want you to come back home so we can start over.' All I can tell you is I was relieved. It was a great feeling."

For the first time in more than a year, Frank and Donna simply talked. They talked openly about their relationship and about forgiveness. They prayed together. Friends at church prayed with them and for them. "It was a long road back, but the talking and praying changed the way we looked at each other," Frank says.

Frank and Donna made it through the rough times and are still married. They raised three kids. Frank is now a church pastor. He believes prayer helped change him even when he wasn't sure he wanted to change. "I can't explain how I changed exactly," he says. "If I could explain that, I could explain God—and I can't do that."

›› Give Hope a Chance

It doesn't necessarily take an act of God to save a marriage (although it can't hurt). But what *does* it take? Let's explore this question because you, like many people contemplating a divorce, may hold to the language and intent of your marriage vows. That is, you may have hope for your marriage. It may be just a glimmer and it may be deep inside, but hope is hope. Divorce counselors, mediators, and attorneys can tick off case after case of troubled marriages that survived after being held together, however tenuously, only by hope.

During a divorce, it is easy and natural to become myopic about your marriage problems. But, for a moment, back up and take a broader perspective. Our society pays a high price for divorce, and many religious and community leaders are working to strengthen marriages and reduce the divorce rate.

In 1940 there were 264,000 divorces in the United States, according to National Center for Health Statistics. By 1992 the number of divorces had reached 1,215,000. The number dropped in 1998 to 1,163,000. Experts say that while divorce rates are decreasing slightly, new marriages in the United States have a 40 to 50 percent chance of ending in divorce. Troubled or torn marriages contribute to social problems such as substance abuse, violent crime, greater incidences of physical and mental disorders, higher health insurance costs, as well as employee absenteeism and lower productivity.

To avoid these problems, many churches offer marriage preparation and enrichment classes. Classes help prepare couples for the realities of marriage and give them time to think twice about marriage. They may come to realize as classic film star Mae West did that "marriage is a great institution, but I'm not ready for an institution yet."

Some clergy and community groups have teamed up to form community marriage policies. For example, couples seeking to marry in Lenawee County, Michigan, must complete a premarital education program before the ceremony. If they do not, the couple can get a marriage license but may have a hard time finding a county official to marry them.

Community marriage policies have had an impact in several cities, according to the American Association for Marriage and Family Therapy. The policies in Modesto, California, helped lower the divorce rate 40 percent between 1986 and 1996. The drop was 18.6 percent from 1991 to 1995 in Peoria, Illinois, and 12 percent from 1993 to 1995 in Montgomery, Alabama.

Law changes

Legislators in some states are working to make divorcing more difficult. Proposed legislation includes making premarital counseling mandatory to obtain a marriage license, a lower license fee and tax breaks for couples attending marriage preparation courses, and delays in obtaining a marriage license for couples who do not do premarital work.

Many states are also considering dumping no-fault divorces and reintroducing fault into divorce proceedings. There are many pros and cons to this controversial proposal. As an optional approach, some states that have no-fault divorce laws are considering a mandatory six-month cooling-off period before divorce papers could be filed.

After reading the previous material, you can see that the business of saving marriages has become the business of more than just the couple. And yet, ultimately, the couple must do the most work to save the marriage. Usually, they cannot work on their problems alone. They need the help of a professional such as a marriage and family therapist. Even Frank, who did not go to a therapist to save his marriage, wishes that he and Donna had done so.

"The only thing I would consider going into debt for is counseling— it is that important to saving marriages," says Frank. "I have friends who are happily into their second marriage, but they wish they would have gone to therapy in their first marriage and known what they know now. They say they would have never gotten a divorce. The counseling helps people get over their immaturity, become adults, and resolve differences. I mean, people think the grass is always greener on the other side of the fence when it comes to marriage. Well, with the help of counseling and such, you learn that the grass is greenest where you water it most."

>> **AFTER AN AFFAIR**

Affairs are painful, embarrassing, humiliating—and common. One 1992 study published in the *Journal of Sex Research* found that 44 percent of husbands and 25 percent of wives had engaged in at least one extramarital sexual experience.

Affairs do not have to mean the end of a marriage. In fact, an affair may serve as a wake-up call for a marriage and help a couple, with the assistance of a therapist, to put the infidelity in perspective, explore underlying marital problems, and learn how to renew the relationship. But this rebuilding takes time—up to two years of biweekly visits with a therapist to reestablish reliability and trust, say some experienced therapists.

The American Association for Marriage and Family Therapy identifies three phases to healing infidelity in therapy:

1. In the first phase, the couple experiences a surge of hope. This lasts about a month or so after the start of marital therapy. With the immediate crisis behind them, the couple feels good about their decision to move on and work on their marriage.

After an Affair continued on next page

>> ## What Can You Do to Save Your Marriage?

The short answer is, plenty. Here are 10 divorce-prevention suggestions that we have gleaned primarily from the world of marriage and family therapy. Our intent is not to provide the "magic bullet" that will miraculously fix your failing marriage. We offer some of the strategies and techniques that therapists use to help struggling couples. What helps some couples may not help others. Therapy is a creative and dynamic process. There are no formulas for preventing divorce. But the bottom line is this: There is help, it often works, and it is only a phone call away.

After an Affair continued from previous page

2. No more secrets, the second phase, takes several months. The therapist helps the couple take a deeper look at the affair and their marriage. The person who had the affair is tested to see if he or she can reveal all the details, which may lead to anger from the spouse, and if he or she can assume full responsibility and not blame the spouse, work pressures, or the like. The person who did not have the affair must work to move past the anger and hurt, and be willing to face his or her role in the underlying marriage problems.

3. In new beginnings, the third and final phase, the therapist helps the couple discover new ways to relate to each other and to revive their sexual relationship. The couple learns new communication skills and methods for resolving conflict. They start "dating" each other again, learning how to enjoy each other's company and negotiate their differences. This is the longest of the three phases, and success is not guaranteed. If the marriage eventually fails, the couple can accept this outcome and then move on to the divorce with a better sense of closure.

1. Record your arguments.

During arguments, couples often say to each other, "You should hear yourself!" It is almost a cliché that these spats break down into the endless back and forth of: "I did not say that!" — "Oh, yes you did!" People don't listen well when they are hot, which can lead to what therapists call "emotional cul-de-sacs" where couples go round and round and get nowhere in resolving disputes.

One solution is to hit the record button on an audiotape recorder while you are arguing and then listen to your arguments. First, you can clear up the facts of who said what. Second, according to therapists, you "get real clean, real fast" knowing that what you say is on tape. You're less likely to shout first and think second because when you play it back, you recognize that you may sound idiotic. Also, in listening to your taped talks, you are just enough removed from the fray to hear what the two of you are trying to say.

2. Remove extended families.

Extended family members often bring even more trouble to troubled marriages. Everyone has advice—even demands—that you should do this or do that.

3. Investigate the realities of divorced life.

Write about what you think your finances, social life, and emotional outlook would be if you were to go through with a divorce. Talk with five people who have divorced, and ask them if their new life is what they expected. Talk with divorce attorneys and mediators, and then ask yourself: "Is this really for me?"

4. Take depression and alcoholism into account.

Sometimes, marriages break down not because the couple cannot get along, but because the couple cannot get past the debilitating diseases of depression and alcoholism. Once the affected spouse (or spouses) receives treatment, the marriage often can survive because the husband and wife are healthy again.

5. Know thyself.

Therapy can help you learn about yourself, your family-of-origin's rules, and your patterns in past relationships. Your rules and patterns may be at odds with those of your spouse, and may be at the root of your conflicts. Once you understand where both you and your spouse are coming from, you can build on the overlap and negotiate the differences.

6. Consider dating . . . your spouse.

Ask yourself: "What was my spouse like when we started dating? Why was I attracted to him or her?" Block out all that has transpired since, and just focus on your feelings then. This will remind you that your spouse is a good person.

Next, go out on dates. Take turns planning them and asking each other out. Try to approach your spouse as if you are attempting to get to know this person as he or she is right now. You may be holding on to old images of each other and may be surprised and fascinated by the person your spouse has grown to be.

7. Call each other twice a day.

Too often, the only contact troubled couples have with each other is at the beginning and end of the day, when each person is either harried or drained by the day. Consequently, they make no real connection with each other. Phone calls during the day are an opportunity to talk when each of you is freshest and removed from your regular duties of home. The calls need not be long, say therapists, just long enough to let your spouse know that you care for him or her and that you are wondering how the day is going. If these calls contain a joke you heard at work or lead to an intimate conversation, all the better.

8. Re-interpret the "D" word.

Divorce therapists and attorneys claim that as many as half of the people who say they want a divorce really don't. Instead they want a major improvement in their marriage. "They really don't want out, they just want power or the ability to vent after years of frustration and being emotionally cut off from each other," says Mark T. Schaefer, Ph.D., who specializes in marriage counseling in his practice at Associated Psychological Consultants in Bloomington, Minnesota.

With this in mind, Schaefer admits he goes into divorce therapy sessions "with a skeptical attitude." He lets his clients know that he is a proponent of marriage. "It is nonsense that I pretend to sit there in neutrality," he says. "I try to help them understand how they got to where they are, and I listen knowing that the family's legacy is at stake. It is with a sense of honor that I am with them at this critical moment in their lives.

"I ask, 'What sense can we make of this?' Then I help them find answers and, hopefully, help them turn around their marriage. If not, I help provide a safe and respectful atmosphere where they can talk and heal. If they choose divorce, they are better able to let go. Sadly, many clients say they wish they would have started therapy years earlier."

9. Look at how your fights end.

You send out truce signals when you want to stop arguing. For instance, your face softens, and you say, "I understand." These signals mark the transition from fighting to getting along. Once you identify these truce signals, try using them more often and earlier in your arguments.

10. Go with what is working.

Therapist Michelle Weiner-Davis, author of the best-selling book *Divorce Busting,* recommends that couples focus on what is different about the times in their life when they are not having problems. She asks each partner to come up with a list of what is different and then analyze that list. This exercise encourages people to not take for granted what *is* working, even if whatever it is seems like a small success. Recognizing little successes, she says, leads to bigger ones because this recognition generates immediate feelings of well-being and hope.

As we mentioned earlier, when we list these techniques, we are not suggesting simple solutions to complex marriage problems. We list them to let you know that marriages can be saved with professional help.

›› Trial Separations

Various studies have shown that roughly one in four couples who consider divorcing will eventually reconcile. A trial separation, in which couples agree to live separately without divorcing, can be an intermediary step that helps you decide if you want to divorce or reconcile. There are two types of trial separations, legal and informal.

The legal separation is less common. It requires a legal document, drawn up in detail by two lawyers, each representing one of you. The process can be as painful and expensive as drafting a contentious divorce agreement—and you will need to go through it all over again if

›› PREDICTING MARITAL SUCCESS

In the early 1990s, therapist John Gottman, Ph.D., boldly went where no one had gone before. Based on studies of nearly 500 couples whom he followed for as long as 10 years, Gottman said that he could predict—with 94 percent accuracy—which marriages were headed for divorce.

To make his predictions, Gottman studied videotapes of the couples, analyzed questionnaires and interviews, and measured physiological data (heart rate, blood-flow rate, perspiration during stress, and even stress-related hormones in urine and blood).

Gottman wrote two books on his studies: *Why Marriages Succeed or Fail,* and *What Predicts Divorce.* Among his findings are the following:

- ▶ *Compatibility.* It isn't the lack of compatibility that predicts a divorce, but the way couples handle their inevitable incompatibilities. Gottman's research says that it is a balance between positive and negative emotional interactions in a marriage that determines its well-being. Satisfied couples were those who maintained a ratio of 5 to 1 of positive to negative moments. This ratio applies to marriages whether they are validating, volatile, or conflict-avoiding.

- ▶ *Four Negatives.* No marriage can last long once four destructive personal exchanges work themselves into a relationship: criticism, defensiveness, contempt, and stonewalling. Gottman found that a husband's contempt in marriage predicted, over time, a wife's susceptibility to illness.

- ▶ *Housework.* Compared with men who do no housework, those who did were likely to be more happily married, less lonely, less stressed, and less susceptible to illness.

- ▶ *Taking Breaks.* Fighting couples are so aroused physiologically that they often are unable to intellectually or emotionally absorb what each other—and therapists—have to say. Therefore, Gottman recommends the couple take a soothing break of at least 20 minutes whenever their pulse rises more than 10 beats per minute over normal during an argument.

you proceed to a divorce. For this reason, most experts recommend an informal separation.

In some cases, however, a legal separation can make sense. For example, if a husband and wife have hugely different incomes, a legal separation allows one spouse to pay tax-deductible alimony to the other. This may be financially advantageous if the couple expects the divorce agreement will take a long time to draft.

An informal separation is a less-structured agreement to live separately for a time.

A trial separation offers these advantages:

- ▶ Allows you to experience many aspects of divorce without being legally divorced
- ▶ Is reversible without the involvement of lawyers and courts
- ▶ May give both parties the chance to reevaluate their own behaviors with separate counselors
- ▶ Allows both spouses to retain shared coverage for medical and other benefits from one spouse's employer.

Separations are especially necessary if there is physical or sexual abuse of either the spouse or children.

We asked John Krumberger, Ph.D., a licensed psychologist in St. Paul, Minnesota, who has worked with couples and children for 21 years, to give us some guidelines on informal separations. "The most important part of a trial separation is its intent," Krumberger says. "Is one spouse using the separation to stall or punish the other? Or is the intent to help each party to work through issues and be clearer about whether they want a divorce? Both people should list what issues they want to address during separation. How are they going to manage the household obligations and the children? Are they going to see marriage counselors? Are they going to date others? All of this needs to be discussed before the trial separation can be fruitful."

One of the most complicated parts of an informal separation involves the decision of who moves out of the home. Should the divorce happen, this decision could influence custody negotiations. We will explore this issue further in the section "Who moves out?" later in this chapter.

›› How to Begin the Ending: A "Divorcing Agreement"

At this point, we are going to assume you and your spouse have done the hard but important emotional work around coming to terms with getting a divorce. We also realize that the decision may change several times before it is final.

How, then, do married couples begin to end their marriage? We have found that a useful first step is to formalize the ending by renegotiating the marriage contract and redefining it as a *divorcing agreement*. In both cases, we are using the term *agreement* in a nonlegal sense.

We're willing to bet that most of you are going to ask one of two immediate questions. First, what is a marriage contract? Second, what if we don't have one? A marriage contract is just that: a written agreement as to what each of you will contribute to the union, and what each of you expects from the other. Most couples we've met don't have a written agreement. Few have a verbal agreement. No wonder they haven't met each other's expectations!

Even if you do not have a marriage contract, you can facilitate your separation and divorce by renegotiating your unwritten—and perhaps unsaid—agreement. This time, put your agreement in writing! Instead of a marriage contract, this becomes a divorcing agreement. The process of writing one may help you work through another step of the divorce process.

It is important to define and respect the needs of each partner during the divorce process. Putting these expectations and agreements on paper will help set the tone for your divorce.

Now, you may ask the obvious question: If we couldn't agree on how to be married, how can we agree on how to be divorced? As we said in chapter 1, a No-Load Divorce is not for everyone. But if you try to follow this process, you may find yourself learning new behaviors of communication that will not only end your marriage respectfully but will also prepare you for new, healthy relationships.

We suggest that the divorcing agreement be in writing and be brief. It should note in the introduction that the "agreement" is not a legal document. The divorcing agreement should outline how you want to behave toward each other on matters crucial to the divorce process. This includes sharing custody of the children as well as dividing property and

›› THE DIVORCING AGREEMENT OUTLINE

▸ **Goals**

In addition to your specific goals, you should include the following statement: Our goals are to reach agreement on how we will conduct ourselves with each other and how we will handle communications, our children, and financial issues while we are divorcing. We strive for mutual respect, fairness, and clarity of expectations. We agree that this document represents an understanding, not a legal agreement.

▸ **Why we are divorcing**

What we agree to tell our children, family, friends, and employers.

▸ **Custody**

How we will raise our children during the divorce process. How much time each of us will spend with the children. How we will handle birthdays, vacations, and school events. How we will handle the children's religious education.

▸ **Careers**

If both spouses work, how we will support each other's career and responsibilities toward the children.

▸ **Sexual relations**

Whether we will continue to be sexual with each other. Whether we will be sexual outside the marriage during the divorce.

▸ **Maintenance**

Whether we will live separately in the same house or in different locations. If we live in the same house, we will assign household duties.

The Divorcing Agreement Outline continued on next page

settling financial issues during the divorce process. See the accompanying sidebar for a sample divorcing agreement outline. The work you do in establishing the divorcing agreement will lay the groundwork for accomplishing the No-Load Divorce agreement.

The Divorcing Agreement Outline continued from previous page

► **Temporary assignment of financial obligations**

We agree on who is responsible for specific credit cards, insurance policies, vehicles, lake homes, current bills, and so on. We agree on who pays day care and educational expenses, and how we will fund taxes and retirement plans. We also agree on whether we will both set up separate checking accounts, and who will manage current investments.

► **Monthly budget**

How much income each party will contribute to jointly agreed-on expenses. We will agree on who will collect the income and make the payments. We will address payments to charities, church/mosque/synagogues, gifts, insurance premiums, and property maintenance. We will agree to share records.

► **Friends and events**

Whom we intend to keep as joint friends, and whom we each want to keep as separate friends. We will agree on events we want to continue to attend as couples and ones to attend separately.

► **Problem solving**

This section outlines a simple process for joint participation in discussions and resolution of future problems.

► **Signatures**

Both parties must sign and date this agreement.

The outline suggests areas that should be addressed. Keep the agreements brief. List them in bullet points. Avoid legal language.

›› When and What to Tell the Children

In our own experience and the experience of our clients going through divorce, nothing is more heartbreaking than dealing with children. They are the most obvious unintended victims. They feel helpless—and they are.

Once you and your partner have decided on a divorce, you need to understand the emotional life of your children in order to know when and what to tell them. Much has been studied and written about how children experience divorce. Their reactions depend on their age, gender, and the amount and duration of conflict in the home before the divorce.

While it is difficult to generalize, a few things seem to be true for all children of divorce. Children are most concerned for how the divorce will affect their lives, and far less focused on your lives. More than likely, they won't want their parents to get divorced, even if they have witnessed open conflict. What they want is an end to the conflict, not an end to the marriage. If there must be a divorce, then they want the least possible disruption to their daily routines.

Above all at this time, children feel out of control. They didn't make the problems between the parents (although sometimes parents blame their children). They know they can't stop their parents from fighting (although some children feel they are responsible). Yet, in the divorce, children see a threat to what they value most: stability, security, and continuity.

Children are going to ask many personal questions when you tell them you are divorcing, and the more answers you have, the better. Here is a list of some of their common questions (we've added space for you to write in answers that you and your partner have agreed on):

► Why are you getting a divorce? _____

_____

_____

_____

► What will happen to my room, and where will I live? _____

_____

_____

_____

► Who will take care of me? _____

_____

_____

_____

▶ How will this affect my school and my friends? _____

_____

_____

_____

▶ What do I tell my friends? _____

_____

_____

_____

▶ How does this affect your love for me? _____

_____

_____

_____

▶ How often will I see you? _____

_____

_____

_____

▶ Will we have enough money to live? _____

_____

_____

_____

▶ Do I get any say in this? _____

_____

_____

_____

"If the ages of the children aren't too far apart, it is best if both parents tell all children at the same time," Krumberger says. "This way, the children hear all the same thing and don't feel they have to take sides. This approach can avoid miscommunication, too, which is easy amid the heightened emotions of divorce."

Krumberger gives some dos and don'ts of what to communicate:

>> **DO**

1. Assure the children they are not responsible.

2. Emphasize that you have plenty of resources to take care of yourself and the family, and that being concerned about having
   enough is not your children's role.

3. Invite the children to share their feelings with you.

>> **DON'T**

1. Grieve in front of your children.

2. Tell your children how angry you are at the other spouse.

3. Ask the children to take sides.

"Kids need to know how their life is going to change," Krumberger says. "Hopefully, it isn't going to change very much. And they're going to want to know why you're getting divorced. Don't go into details. Keep the explanation simple. Just say you're not getting along. You're not happy. You've tried to work it out and can't."

Most parents are racked with guilt over how the divorce has hurt their children. We would like to tell you that children of divorce do fine, but many studies have shown those children bear emotional scars. Children of divorced parents often experience more depression, learning problems, intense anger, sexual promiscuity, and delinquent behavior. Studies have shown that about one out of four children of divorces experience these problems within the first year-and-a-half of divorce. Usually, it gets worse before it gets better. By three years after the divorce, the fraction increases to about one-third. Then adjustment and emotional problems seem to subside as children age, particularly if parents create and maintain stability and a nurturing environment.

In most cases, children eventually improve after the divorce if the divorce results in fewer conflicts between the parents.

›› CHANGES IN YOUR RELATIONSHIP WITH YOUR CHILDREN

Even when you have shared custody, there will be times when you must get used to:

1. Having to ask for time with your own children

2. Not tucking your children into bed at night

3. Not knowing if your children are sick

4. Knowing your children are sick but not being able to care for them because they are at the other parent's house

5. Not seeing your children on their birthdays

6. Not seeing your children on your birthday

7. Having to give up your children in the middle of a holiday, such as Christmas

8. Transferring clothes

9. Coordinating homework

10. Seeing your ex-spouse at school events and games when your children are on teams

11. Coordinating parent-teacher conferences

12. Dealing with your ex-spouse's new husband or wife

13. Watching your ex-spouse's new husband or wife influence your children

›› Who Moves Out?

Deciding who moves out can be one of the first and yet most difficult decisions of the divorce process. The decision is difficult on two levels. On an emotional level, the person who moves out has to set up new living arrangements and will leave behind the emotional security of familiar surroundings. What makes the decision most difficult, however, is that on a practical level, moving out may have an impact on custody decisions.

Generally, the primary consideration of a divorce court is for children to have continuing and frequent contact with both parents. With this in mind, the parent who moves out must try to arrange contact with the children in a way that causes the least disruption and the most opportunity for contact.

Here are some guidelines:

Children like equal time with their parents.

Most children do not want to take sides in a divorce and prefer to spend equal amounts of time with each parent. The court likes to see that this is the case, because it shows that both parents are equally vested in raising the children.

Children will want to stay in their own rooms in the family home.

The spouse who moves out may not be able to afford a home where there are enough bedrooms to accommodate the children. Even if there are enough bedrooms, the spouse needs to buy beds and some furniture. Then the child or children need to be given time to get used to living in two places. However, setting up a similar, stable environment in two places is possible and often happens.

Children must go to one school.

If you move to a home outside of the children's school area, you must drive the children to and from school.

Children like to be near their friends.

If you move too far from your family home, it may be difficult for your children to maintain their school and neighborhood friendships.

While there is no legal penalty for moving out, the decision can ultimately influence the final court-ordered custody situation. Some lawyers even suggest that before one spouse moves out, the couple enter into a binding, written agreement with respect to custody and parenting time with the children. Lawyers say the agreement should be filed in court as a consent order.

Without a clear agreement, legal or informal, the spouse who moves out could be sending an unintended message that the children aren't important. The spouse who stays in the home might resist, for any number of reasons, letting the children spend time with the spouse who moved out. The spouse who moves out must move into a home that provides reasonable room for the children, or the court may again interpret the move as not being in the children's interest.

If the spouse who moves out establishes a pattern of seeing the children less frequently than the spouse who remains in the home, the judge may view the spouse at home as the primary parent. Judges tend to support a status quo custody order, giving the spouse who moved out less time with the children on a permanent basis.

›› Facing the Financial Consequences of Divorce

The financial impact of divorce can be as powerful and distressing as the emotional impact. You need to be aware of the potential costs.

Above all, always keep in mind this rule: The more conflict between you and your spouse during the divorce process, the more the divorce will cost. One of our primary motivations in writing this book is to offer an alternative way to reach a divorce settlement that can dramatically reduce the financial costs.

First, let's consider the typical costs in a contentious divorce. Each party begins the process by hiring an attorney. Each attorney charges by the hour, and the rates can range from $150 to $300 an hour, depending on the attorney's experience. Most attorneys require that you "retain" them, which means that you must send them between $3,000 and $5,000 before they begin to work with you. Their first bills are deducted from the retainer. After the retainer is spent, you will begin to receive monthly bills for their time and expenses.

Attorneys charge for everything that affects their time. If you call your attorney to complain about what your spouse did, you get charged for time on the phone, time they needed to research your question, and time to call or write you with further information. When your attorney and your spouse's attorney talk or negotiate, both you and your spouse get charged for the time. You get charged for filing interrogatories and motions, for scheduling meetings, and for research and preparation time related to your case. You will be charged for drafts of agreements and renegotiations of those agreements. You will be charged for time in court and transit time for the attorney.

If your divorce is contentious, legal bills can average $25,000 per person. Legal fees in bitter divorces can cost up to $50,000 (or more) per person.

Beyond legal costs, you and your spouse will have other expenses. If one of you rents an apartment, the cost will have to come from your combined household income. The spouse who moves out may need to purchase furniture and other household items. Sometimes the stay-at-home spouse goes back to school or takes a job, and child-care costs can increase significantly.

If you follow the No-Load Divorce, you and your spouse will do much of the negotiating together and with the help of a mediator. Mediators charge between $50 and $150 an hour. A non-contentious mediation may take about 5 to 10 one-hour sessions. Total mediation costs should average $1,000. If each of you hires a No-Load Divorce lawyer, the mediated agreement can be reviewed, amended, and agreed on for about $1,000 per lawyer, or $2,000 total. Including the presentation in court and final distribution of the court order, your total costs for a No-Load Divorce can average $3,000, compared to a contentious divorce, which can cost $50,000 or more.

›› An Agreement to Start the No-Load Divorce

The biggest step you will take in this book is to agree with your spouse to a No-Load Divorce. As a result of the work you have done in this chapter, you have clarified your emotions and the issues. You have sought advice and counseling. You may have tried a trial separation or be ready for it. You are reconciled or emotionally ready to follow through with the divorce and understand the financial and emotional consequences. You have agreed on some behaviors to follow during the divorce by drafting a divorcing agreement.

This may be the time to commit to the No-Load Divorce process.

We asked Lois Egan, a Minneapolis marriage psychotherapist, how a couple can formally reach this commitment. "The couple should start with a formal emotional ending," she says. "And this involves three stages."

1. The first stage is to suspend blame.

"Lots of times during marriage, couples won't say what they honestly feel and want," Egan says. "They may be afraid their needs would put too much stress on the marriage. Ironically, this lack of honesty often causes a marriage to fail. Each spouse wants to blame the other. So the first step is for both to relinquish blame and do this in front of each other."

2. The second stage involves a review of lost dreams.

Egan asks couples to share with each other the dreams they had for the relationship that weren't realized and are never going to be.

3. The last stage is to list what you had together and didn't have together.

"As emotionally difficult as this is," Egan says, "it frees you to refocus from a place of revenge and anger to a place of dignity. Now you can end the marriage and begin to think about what is best for each of you and your children."

Most couples are angry because they blame the marriage for making their lives miserable. "In truth," Egan says, "almost always the conflict was inherited by the marriage and not caused by the marriage."

These issues are often heart wrenching and difficult to examine, especially at a time when you feel vulnerable and in transition. Give yourself credit for having the courage to examine your decisions and look inward at your real motivations.

We began this chapter by asking, "Are you sure it's over?" We hope what we presented in the beginning of the chapter has helped you discover that, indeed, your marriage is not over and that, with work, it will continue as an even stronger marriage. But we are also realistic. We understand that marriages end. If that is the case, we hope we have offered information that will help you end the marriage respectfully, and that you both will become ready to commit to the No-Load Divorce.

CHAPTER 3

Divorce 101: What You Need to Know— Starting Now

Beth was shoveling her driveway in the middle of a blizzard on Halloween in 1991. The weather system that would lead to the Sebastian Junger book and movie *The Perfect Storm* was dumping 30 inches of snow on the Midwest.

As the snow kept falling, Beth was feeling snowed under in more ways than one. The next day her husband would move out under court order. In September of that year, she had begun divorce proceedings by contacting an attorney and a counselor—for herself, not for them as a couple. After 20 years of tension, she had had enough. She had become increasingly afraid for her safety and that of her four children because of her husband's domineering and, more recently, threatening behavior. He would wander through the house waving a gun for no reason, claiming he was going to clean it. He had used a cleaver to destroy a credit card. When he threw a large glass of juice in Beth's face, she called 911.

Back then, Beth knew nothing about the ground rules of settlement and divorce. She was overwhelmed. Financial problems loomed as a result of the upcoming divorce. She was trying to sell the house, but she had no offers after 180 showings. Beth and her spouse each had lawyers to pay, and the proceedings had quickly become adversarial and, consequently, expensive. She had no friends of her own because all were really *their* friends, and Beth did not know whose side their friends were taking. The kids were a mess. She was depressed. And her driveway was filling with snow.

"I had no knowledge of divorce," recalls Beth. "None of my friends or family members had gone through a divorce or even any sort of legal proceedings, so I did not know about lawyers, custody, alimony, joint parenting—anything."

Most people who seek divorce are as clueless as Beth was. They do what they think they should do: hire a lawyer immediately. This is often an expensive and incorrect move, as we will see in Beth's case.

Yet looking back on the divorce, many people often say they wish someone would have answered basic questions before the process seemed to take on a roller-coaster life of its own. Some people recall being so in the dark that they wish someone would have told them *what questions* to ask.

›› Getting You Up to Speed

Our goal in this chapter is to get you up to speed on the ground rules of settlement and divorce. We know you have a lot on your mind, so we are not going to belabor this topic. We are going to quickly but thoroughly walk you through a typical divorce and give you simple guidelines so you won't be blindsided during the proceedings, lose out on matters that are important to you, and then throw up your hands and walk away from the divorce with a Steven Seagal attitude. You may recall this macho actor's quote after his divorce: "Instead of getting married again, I'm going to find a woman I don't like and just give her a house."

Many lawyers seem to assume their divorcing clients know the process and options. Unless you ask, you may not be told. As we reported in chapter 1, Bill's lawyer did not tell him about mediation, a basic and essential option in the divorcing process, until Bill asked.

Being in the dark about these ground rules and being too quick to "let the lawyers handle it" can be costly and unsatisfying. Beth called an attorney friend, who recommended three lawyers to interview for her divorce. Beth felt she needed a lawyer because her husband had already hired two to plead his case. Beth interviewed the three candidates and chose the one with a "good-but-tough" reputation. In explaining her case to the lawyer, Beth found herself searching for a sympathetic listener and not finding one. "Most attorneys-at-law are not counselors, so don't use your time with them as an opportunity to vent," she says. "My lawyer would cut me off as I explained my situation, and she was kind of rude. It was strictly 'stick to the facts.'"

Some attorneys, unlike Beth's stick-to-the-facts lawyer, actually encourage their clients to talk about their emotional needs, even though

›› UNITED STATES DIVORCE STATISTICS

Total divorces:	**1,163,000**
US rate:	**4.1 per 1000 people**
Nevada rate (highest):	**9.0 per 1000 people**
Massachusetts rate (lowest):	**2.4 per 1000 people**
Number of divorced adults in US	**19.4 million**
Median age of divorce:	**Males—35.6**
	Females—33.2
Median duration of marriage	**7.2 years**
Percentage of first marriages ending in divorce	**50%**
Average length of divorce proceedings	**1 year**
Number of children affected by new divorces each year	**1 million**
In 1996, children of divorce were more likely to divorce than children from intact families	**50%**
In 19 reporting states, percentage of custody awarded to the wife	**72%**
awarded to the husband	**9%**

Statistics are from the National Center for Health Statistics. Figures are from the most recent period—1998—unless otherwise stated.

the attorneys are not professional counselors. Perhaps these lawyers think they are being helpful. But they do bill for this time, and it may not be productive. Bill spent four hours with his attorney at $300 an hour talking about his emotional state. This exhausted half of Bill's retainer and was of no legal benefit to him.

The more Beth talked with her lawyer, the more unsettled she became. "I wanted to be a good person as well as win the case. But my attorney told me right up front that we were going to play hardball. So, the tone of the legal papers was shrill and harsh. I did not recognize myself in those papers. However, my friends told me to suck it up and follow the advice of the paid professional. They said this must be how the legal system works, and no one reads this stuff anyway."

The big issue in Beth's divorce was joint custody, which we will explain in more detail later in this chapter. But the bottom line in Beth's case is this: She "won." It took her nearly two years and $20,000 to get the custody she wanted, but she won.

"It was astounding how much money I spent," says Beth. "I did not understand how long it would take and that the wheels of justice turn slowly. I didn't understand a lot of things. I simply took the attorney's advice. I did not read any books on how divorce works. I was just told to do this or do that, and I did it."

You are going to hear from Beth later, in chapter 6, because, unfortunately, Beth and her ex locked horns again a decade after the divorce. This second costly legal confrontation could have been avoided had the concept of No-Load Divorce been available then and had this couple signed on to it.

›› Who Files First for Divorce?

Theoretically, it shouldn't matter who files for divorce. In practical terms, however, many attorneys say the person who files first has some advantages. (Remember, the moment you file you may be creating an adversarial situation, unless you and your spouse have pre-negotiated agreements.) Typically, you file at the court in the county where you live.

"In a divorce where there is the potential for a legal battle, I urge my client to file first," says David Harrison, the Rochester, Michigan, divorce attorney we have quoted in previous chapters. "This allows us to set the tone and to some degree control the timing of the initial orders. The other party is put on the defensive because he or she must respond to the charges in the complaint."

Legal terms vary from state to state, but the common term for the legal paper you file is a *complaint for divorce*. A typical complaint includes the reason for divorce (most states accept "irreconcilable differences") and facts about children, residences, and property. The complaint then requests temporary actions. Such actions may include that the other spouse move out of the home, the children stay in the home, current assets be frozen, and custody during the divorce proceedings be handled in a specified way.

The non-filing spouse is given a period of time to respond to the complaint. The responding spouse can agree with the requests or petition the court to change certain requests or orders in the complaint. If there is disagreement, the court holds a hearing. Thus the dispute resolution process begins.

In a No-Load Divorce, in which each spouse agrees to work cooperatively, it doesn't matter who files first. "No one is asking for extreme relief, and you may not need any temporary orders," Harrison says. "Basically, you're both maintaining the marital status quo during the divorce process."

In No-Load Divorce cases, Harrison asks for two things. "First, I ask the couple to agree to leave all assets as they were and pay bills as they did before the divorce complaint," he says. "Second, I ask that both parents deal with the children as they always have. In a noncontested situation, this approach causes the least amount of disruption or defensiveness."

›› The Legal Process

The legal process depends on whether the divorce is one of conflict or one of mutual consent and cooperation, as in the No-Load Divorce. Two other factors that affect this process are (1) whether you begin divorce proceedings, or (2) start with a legal separation (in which case you are still married). We'll assume that the process does not include a legal separation.

In terms of time and money, the differences between a divorce with conflict and a No-Load Divorce are huge. "These are generalities, but I'd put it this way," says Harrison. "When there is conflict over custody, assets, and who lives where, you could be looking at a 6- to 18-month process and legal fees of up to $25,000 per spouse. In a No-Load Divorce situation, the process would take three months [some states may have additional waiting periods] at most and cost from $500 to $1,000 per attorney."

Let's take a closer look at the legal process with conflict and with a No-Load Divorce approach. As you read, pay attention to why the difference in time, money, and emotional stress is so great. Keep in mind that each state has its own legal terms, so your case may be slightly different. But by reading the scenarios below, you'll get a good idea of why we strongly advise a No-Load Divorce.

Divorces with conflict

Typically, in this type of divorce, spouse A files for divorce. The complaint alleges accusations against spouse B. The intent of the accusations is to justify a request for immediate temporary orders placing the children in spouse A's custody. If the couple has no children, the intent is to allow spouse A to gain control of the legal process and put spouse B on the defensive. The complaint also specifies visitation rights, some property assignments, child support amounts, and temporary alimony. Papers are served to spouse B, who has two to four weeks to respond.

Spouse B objects and requests (files a motion for) a hearing. Both spouses present their case at the hearing, but they can't agree on a number of issues. The court then has to settle the differences and lay out the terms of the temporary order. Usually, neither spouse gets what he or she wants.

Then for at least three months, the couple goes through the discovery process. This means that each spouse requests information of the other. The requests are in the form of interrogatories (questions) or subpoenas (requests for documents). During this time, spouses or their attorneys also request appraisals of property.

If the discovery process involves the children, spouses can request school records, independent psychological evaluations, and witness depositions. During discovery, the court may assign someone to mediate disputes.

Motions and arguments in court can be as often as weekly. They can be about important or petty matters in the divorce. Attorney Harrison says he has seen motions about who takes junior to Boy Scouts! It could take a year for the spouses to come to an agreement on all the terms of divorce. This agreement is called a judgment of divorce. If the parties can't reach an agreement, they must go to trial. The case is heard before a civil judge or a representative of that judge, often called a referee or mediator. Each side can call witnesses, and there are accusations, defenses, and counteraccusations. (To get a fairly good idea of these trials, think of television court dramas!) Finally, after a lot of back and forth, the court decides the issues.

What is the aftermath? Spouse A and spouse B usually end up hating each other. The children are miserable and have deeply torn loyalties. No one gets all that he or she wanted. Any sort of cooperation or co-parenting going forward seems impossible. Oh, yes, the attorneys walk away with huge fees.

No-Load Divorces

Spouse A and spouse B give thought to the issues, complete the No-Load Divorce agreement, and desire a respectful divorce experience. They agree that spouse A should file for divorce. The complaint contains no surprises.

Spouse B responds to the complaint with an answer that both spouses have agreed on in advance. If children are involved, the court may require a waiting period, in case there is any chance for reconciliation. Meanwhile, a judgment of divorce is drafted incorporating the agreements of the two spouses. The judgment of divorce is submitted to the court. After the waiting period, either or both spouses can attend the hearing. Seeing that the two parties have reached agreement, the judge signs the judgment, and the divorce is final.

›› Custody

Custody refers to the living arrangements of the children, that is, where they live and who is responsible for them. Custody involves the responsibility for children until they reach adult age, which in most cases is age 18. Children can be placed in the sole custody of either parent or in joint custody, in which parents share custody.

Temporary custody may be different from the permanent custody arrangements. "Permanent" really means custody starting with the signing of the divorce papers. In the view of the court, however, there is no such thing as "permanent." A permanent custody arrangement can always be modified by court order.

Legal custody refers to the right to make critical decisions about the child's upbringing, such as regarding their medical care, religion, and schooling. Legal custody may be sole or joint. Sole legal custody gives the authority to one parent. Joint legal custody, which most courts favor, requires both parents to agree on these key issues. Once legal custody is set, it is very difficult to change unless there are serious issues such as child abuse or neglect.

Physical custody refers to where the children live. There are three types. Sole physical custody means the children live with one parent. The other parent typically has scheduled times to be with the children, and the arrangement is called visitation rights. Joint physical custody means the children live with each parent roughly half time. Split physical custody refers to arrangements in which the children live full time with one parent part of the year and full time with the other parent part of the year. Split physical custody also refers to arrangements in which some of the children live with one parent, and some live with the other.

›› ADVANTAGES OF JOINT PHYSICAL CUSTODY

We strongly believe that, whenever possible, a divorcing couple should strive for joint physical custody. Here's why:

- Equal parenting time and influence on the children's attitudes and beliefs
- Equal involvement of parents in school activities, sports, hobbies, religious upbringing, and so on
- Opportunity for children to maintain close relationships with both parents
- Association of home with both Mom and Dad
- Discipline and other rules maintained as part of the normal relationship with children; that is, children do not develop a sense of being "on vacation" with one parent
- Sense of security for children because of their relationships with both parents.

›› Visitation Schedules

In cases in which physical custody is awarded to one parent, the noncustodial parent may receive visitation rights. Visitation rights may be "reasonable" or "fixed."

Reasonable visitation is largely at the discretion of the parent with sole physical custody. In most cases, courts prefer fixed visitation. This is visitation assigned at particular times of the week.

›› Child Support Payments

Child support payments are monthly payments from the noncustodial parent to the custodial parent. In some cases in which the custodial parent is the primary wage earner, the noncustodial parent may not be required to make child support payments. These payments are court ordered and meant to help maintain the health and welfare of the children. Each state has guidelines for calculating a range of child support to be paid, based on the parents' incomes and expenses. These guidelines can vary considerably from state to state.

›› Alimony

Alimony, sometimes called spousal maintenance, is meant to compensate a spouse for a discrepancy in earning power caused by the marriage. Women are more likely than men to have sacrificed career advancement for child rearing. When women get divorced and their income is not supplemented by alimony, they usually see a dramatic decline in their standard of living. Alimony is meant to help prevent such a dramatic decline. It takes the form of a cash payment made from the ex-spouse who is working or earning a higher wage to the other ex-spouse. Alimony can be paid as a lump sum or in a monthly amount. If certain criteria are met, the alimony payments are tax-deductible for the payer and taxable income for the recipient. Alimony may be ordered until the receiving spouse acquires training or education and a higher-paying job. In some cases, it is paid until the receiving spouse remarries or dies.

›› Property Distribution

Typically, marital assets are split 50:50. Marital assets are assets that build up after the marriage (and may not include inheritances). We'll cover property distribution in great detail in chapters 5 and 7.

You can obtain a personalized, sample settlement proposal on our Web site (www.noloaddivorce.com), which will address property distribution, child support guidelines, and recommended alimony payments for your situation. See Appendix A for three examples of settlements.

›› How Much Will a Divorce Cost?

The cost of a divorce depends on the complexity of the issues and how well the divorcing couple can come to agreement. Usually, the simpler the case, the less the cost. Cases are made more complicated when there are children, large property settlements, or business ownership involved.

Divorce attorneys generally charge between $150 and $300 an hour. Price does not necessarily reflect an attorney's experience or ability. A divorce with limited property settlement issues and no children could cost between $1,000 and $5,000. When children are involved or the couple contests many property and support matters, the costs can be more than $30,000 per person. The estimated average cost of a divorce in the United States is $15,000, according to the National Center for Health Statistics.

›› How Long Does It Take to Get Divorced?

According to the National Center for Health Statistics, the average time to obtain a divorce is one year. However, with custody disputes, interrogatories, and hearings, the divorce process could take up to two years.

›› The No-Load Divorce Ground Rules

Now that we've gone over the issues and process of divorce, let's look at the No-Load Divorce ground rules. These ground rules, found on the following two pages, are our practical suggestions for moving the divorce along at a reasonable pace and ending it with reasonable results.

Remember the No-Load Divorce and these ground rules work best for couples who have come to terms with the divorce and who have the emotional support they need to be fair as they move forward. The irony is that couples who are bitter, angry, and vengeful as they begin the divorce process will, in most cases, end up following these rules anyway—but only after months (or years) of emotional turmoil and huge legal fees. Most cases end up being mediated after 6 to 24 months—and after legal fees have mounted. When all is said and done, the case is usually settled based on state guidelines, as it would have been in the first place with less time, money, and aggravation.

›› THE NO-LOAD DIVORCE GROUND RULES

These ground rules apply to divorcing couples who want to partici-
pate in raising their children. We also assume there are not com-
plicating factors, such as suspected child or spousal abuse, mental
illness, and the like.

1. *Custody*. Whenever possible, joint legal custody is in the
   best interest of the children because it allows for the input
   of both parents and keeps both parents involved. If you're
   both committed to co-parenting equally, joint physical
   custody is preferred. If only one parent has the time and
   inclination to care for the children the majority of time,
   typically there will be an arrangement in which there is
   joint legal custody, and the parent providing the majority
   of care will have physical custody with visitation rights for
   the other parent.

2. *Child support*. When there is a discrepancy in the incomes
   of the parents and in the time the children spend in one
   household over the other, the noncustodial parent should
   expect (and want) to pay child support. States and counties have specific guidelines. Accept them.

3. *Alimony*. If you make more money than your ex-spouse
   makes, you may be required to provide spousal support.
   This could include paying for your ex-spouse to get the
   training and education required for a higher-paying job
   (unless the ex-spouse is raising the children). States and
   counties have alimony guidelines. Pay the alimony according to these guidelines.

4. *Property distribution*. Laws vary by state, but generally, what
   you bring into the marriage is yours. What you accumulate during the marriage should be split 50:50. Make sure
   each person is left with some cash and not just property.
   We'll discuss guidelines for typical property distribution
   settlements in chapter 5.

The No-Load Divorce Ground Rules continued on next page

The No-Load Divorce Ground Rules continued from previous page

5. ***Joint parenting.*** You're going to have to negotiate with your ex-spouse consistently as you jointly raise your children. You'll be transferring the children and their things back and forth for years to come. It won't always be easy. Expect this and make any critical comments about your ex-spouse out of your children's hearing.

6. ***Timing.*** The divorce should take no more than one year if (1) you cooperate with your ex-spouse, use goodwill, and avoid interrogatories, custody studies, and other legal squabbles; and (2) if you follow these ground rules and use the No-Load Divorce process and agreement.

For an informal pre-divorce settlement proposal involving your situation and for the purposes of outlining child support, alimony, and property distribution, go to www.noloaddivorce.com.

CHAPTER 4

Negotiating Nicely and Finding Professional Help

Frankly, we love this topic, and it shows by the number of negotiating tips we will give you in this chapter. Negotiation is at the bedrock of much of life, including business, relationships, and certainly divorces. There is power in negotiation. "Diplomacy is the art of letting someone else have your way," said Italian diplomat Daniele Vari.

Beyond power, there is tremendous satisfaction in negotiation. You identify what you want, stand up for it, and (if you negotiate right) help someone else get what he or she wants as well. In a word, negotiating well will help you have a good divorce—as opposed to the divorce that comes out in this bit of humor from Robin Williams: "Ah yes, divorce . . . from the Latin word meaning to rip out a man's genitals through his wallet."

>> The Art of Negotiation

Many couples heading into divorce have never learned to negotiate. This is unfortunate because they will be called on to undertake some of the most difficult compromises ever, at a time of high emotions and mistrust.

When you select a No-Load Divorce mediator (see below), the mediator will involve you in a process that encourages negotiation. There probably are as many different processes of negotiation as there are mediators. No one process of negotiation is better than another—except the process that works best for you. The message here is that you may need to experiment to find the process that fits your personality.

To be productive, negotiation requires that both parties are willing to look for common ground and will not hide information or assets. Ideally, the goal is not to produce a winner and a loser. Negotiation results in either a winner and a winner (a satisfying conclusion for both parties) or a loser and a loser. You are attempting to discover what makes a good result for you and what constitutes a good result for your spouse. To do this, you need to be well prepared, alert, and flexible.

Here's a five-step negotiation process you could try, perhaps in preparation for your first meetings with your mediator. Feel free to modify this one as you wish or develop your own. The important thing is that as you begin negotiating, you begin to visualize gains, not losses. The more you work out your own method of negotiating, the more confidence and less fear you will have—which will make you all the more effective. John F. Kennedy once said something we believe to be so true: "Let us never negotiate out of fear, but let us never fear to negotiate."

›› A Five-Step Negotiation Process

Step 1: Make a list.

Each spouse should start by writing down a list of what he or she wants. Do this separately, before discussing anything. Use the chapter 7 worksheets, which are also available at www.noloaddivorce.com. Cover as many issues and possessions as possible, including custody arrangements, child support, the house, furniture, cars, and so on. Remember, child support follows guidelines that vary by state or county. You can get this information from your county social service agency, a mediator, or our Web site.

"Usually, couples surprise each other when they compare lists and find some areas of agreement they wouldn't have imagined," says Lynn Lott, a marriage and family therapist from Richmond, California. "The fear is that one spouse will ask for the kids, house, cars, and furniture, and then wants the other spouse to live out of a suitcase under a bridge. But usually, there is a more natural fairness—and there needs to be for No-Load Divorce to work."

Step 2: Brainstorm.

After you and your spouse compare lists and find areas of agreement, do some brainstorming on how to give up some things in order to get other things in return. This isn't always easy, but you may be pleasantly surprised at how flexible your soon-to-be ex-spouse can be.

Don't be surprised, however, when you discover logjams. "I had one very wealthy couple in a mediation session, and I was dreading arguments over all the money," Lott says. "Actually, dividing up cars, bonds, diamonds, and vacation homes was easy for them. However, neither of them would budge when it came to who got the two cats! The argument turned bitter. They looked at me. I shrugged and said, 'Ask the cats.'"

Step 3: Celebrate the small victories.

Just remember this: Each agreement you make together—big or small—is one that doesn't need to be mediated, discussed with lawyers, or presented to the court. Put another way, each agreement you make saves you money that would otherwise go to mediators and lawyers. These agreements are your mutual decisions. They should give you some degree of confidence that it is possible for you and your spouse to work together and control the outcome. So, take heart even in small steps forward. When you reach an impasse, take a breather. Let a few days pass. Maybe more ideas will come to each of you so that another agreement will fall into place.

Step 4: Gather more information.

Help is for the asking as you negotiate detail after detail of the divorce. Pick up the phone and start gathering information. That way, you don't have to reinvent the wheel to reach an agreement on each detail.

"I had a couple who couldn't agree on how to handle their membership in the health club," Lott says. "Their assumption was that the membership would go to one and not the other. I suggested that they call the club. Sure enough, the club had many divorced members and had a policy and procedures in place so that each spouse received individual memberships during a cooling-off period."

Step 5: Know when to quit.

When negotiations seem to be stuck, don't keep pushing. Let time work its magic. Try to be patient and to remain creative as you try to agree on issues. Also, remain open to the fact that the agreement you have reached may be the best you can do. It may be time to end negotiations on a particular issue and move on.

Lott says this ending time is when people feel most vulnerable. People may feel that they should have tried harder or been smarter or tried this tactic or that during the negotiations. They may doubt themselves and feel that they "lost." But Lott reminds them that everybody—including your spouse—feels like they lose in a divorce. "Nobody feels it was fair or they got what they deserved. I tell them if you're going to keep on fighting for 'fair,' forget it. 'Fair' doesn't exist. Give yourself a pat on the back and go on to a new day."

›› Selecting Your No-Load Divorce Team

Now we are going to help you select your No-Load Divorce team. This group of handpicked professionals will provide emotional support and expert guidance as you begin negotiating. These professionals include a counselor or counselors, mediator, financial adviser, and two lawyers. All of these professionals subscribe to the No-Load Divorce philosophy.

›› Selecting Counselors and Other Emotional Support

The next step in the No-Load Divorce process is to select a counselor or counselors. Counselors provide emotional support as you face the trauma of divorce. Clergy, spiritual counselors, marriage and family therapists, psychologists, other mental health professionals, and school counselors are available to help.

Ideally, you already have a therapist in place and have used him or her to help save your marriage or come to terms with the divorce. Many therapists want to see the divorcing couple together, so they can get their own picture of the relationship. Therefore, some divorcing couples do joint therapy during the divorce. At the same time, each spouse may choose to do individual therapy with the couple's therapist or with a dif-

▶ *Negotiating Tip #1*

FIGURE OUT WHY YOU HAVE TROUBLE ASKING FOR WHAT YOU WANT.

Asking for what you want is not always easy, especially in divorce negotiations. The following is a simple, two-part exercise that will help you as you ask for what you want during negotiations. The first part is to simply give five reasons why it is so difficult to ask for what you want.

1. _____

2. _____

3. _____

4. _____

5. _____

Most people look at their answers and wince. There is pain in admitting that they find it difficult to ask because they won't get it anyway, they don't deserve it, or they are afraid of being rejected. However, our point is that we want you to be aware of unconscious or unexamined fears about negotiations.

The second part of this exercise is to examine those fears. Is it *really* true that you won't get what you ask for anyway, or that you don't deserve what you want? Cross-examine yourself, and challenge your fears. Perhaps have a trusted friend do the questioning. You may find that your fears are phony or at least not as big a deal as you once believed.

ferent one. Children may benefit from family therapy, even after the divorce. Therapists say that all family members involved in a divorce may need to continue scheduling therapy sessions as the realities of the divorce settle in and as the family continues to face difficult decisions.

The best way to select professional help is by way of referral from a friend, neighbor, co-worker, or your clergy. Some county social service agencies have referral services. United Way offers a First Call for Help phone line. You can also talk with your doctor or other health professionals. Many family practitioners work with a team of providers, including psychologists and therapists, and can refer you to one they know and trust. You can consult the department of psychology at a local college or university, or the local community mental health center.

Several professional organizations can help you find a therapist. The American Psychological Association is one. By calling 1-800-964-2000, you can be connected directly to the state or local referral service for your area. Another is the American Association for Marriage and Family Therapy. Contact AAMFT at 1133 15th Street, NW, Suite 300, Washington, D.C., 20005-2710. Or call 202-452-0109. Check directories for current phone numbers and addresses.

Once you have your short list of therapists who may be right for you, make an appointment to interview them. Ask many questions, including:

- ▸ Are you licensed? What are your credentials? How long have you been practicing?

- ▸ What areas do you specialize in (i.e., family therapy, marriage counseling, etc.)?

- ▸ What kind of treatment do you usually use, and why do you feel this would be effective for my situation? How long would you expect my treatment to last?

- ▸ What are your fees? Will you accept my insurance or HMO coverage? Will you directly bill my insurance company? Do you have a sliding fee scale, or will you set up a payment plan?

Remember that therapy styles are as different as the therapist. Since you are hiring the counselor, you are the customer in charge. Make sure the counselor's style and approach feels right. You should know this after the first session or two. Your treatment will involve working together as partners, and therefore, a good rapport with your counselor is critical. If it is not a match, move on quickly to another one. You want a counselor who is within your price range, responsive to your needs, and flexible enough to meet your schedule.

▸ *Negotiating Tip #2*

AVOID THREE COMMON REACTIONS TO AN ATTACK

Unfortunately, attacks are all too common in divorce negotiations. Attacks invariably amount to one spouse acting before thinking, and then the other spouse reacting in kind. Remember Ambrose Bierce's words: "Speak when you are angry and you will make the best speech you will ever regret."

You should also remember these three don'ts when reacting to attack:

1. ***Don't fight fire with fire.*** Once in a while, you may show your spouse that two can do this dance, which will make him or her stop. But this may be a ploy to draw you into a trap. Your response-in-kind may provide your spouse with a justification for his or her unreasonable behavior. It may also cause an escalation in a game of hardball—a game that you don't want to play.

2. ***Don't wilt.*** You may be tempted to give in after an attack, just to have the negotiation done with. Don't do it. You will kick yourself the next morning. First, the outcome would be unsatisfactory. Second, you are rewarding your spouse for bad behavior. And third, you are in effect telling your spouse that your weakness may be exploited in the future.

3. ***Don't break it off.*** We understand that you may have to end negotiations when your spouse is being utterly impossible. But often breaking off negotiations is a throw-up-your-arms, hasty reaction that you may regret later. Give the matter some time. Ask questions to see if you are misinterpreting your spouse's comments or behavior. Also, keep in mind that breaking it off can become habit-forming, which means you may be too quick to do this in all your negotiating and will never end up with what you want.

›› Choosing a No-Load Divorce Mediator

A mediator is a trained professional who helps couples work together to sort out a wide range of divorce issues and come to agreement on custody and property divisions. While a counselor will help you emotionally as you address custody, property division, and other issues, a mediator is trained to complete the negotiations. In the No-Load-Divorce process, it is essential that you hire a mediator that adheres to No-Load Divorce principles. We recommend one mediator per couple.

Locate mediators using our Web site. Our mediators have met these criteria:

- They are trained in the No-Load Divorce process and agree to follow that process.
- They have agreed to use the No-Load Divorce worksheet found in chapter 7 of this book.
- They have agreed to charge a set fee.

If a mediator is not available in your area, here are some tips on how to select the right mediator. First, you need a referral. We suggest you check:

- Friends
- The Yellow Pages, under "Divorce" or "Mediation"
- Electronic directories available on the World Wide Web. Check the Association for Conflict Resolution, which includes the Academy of Family Mediators.
- Your family court system (see your local White Pages)
- Your counselor or clergy.

When you consider hiring a mediator, ask the mediator to explain his or her credentials and the number of divorces he or she has mediated. Ask for references, and then call at least two. Most mediators are lawyers or counselors. Neither of the two No-Load Divorce lawyers selected by you and your spouse should also serve as mediator. Once you have narrowed your search, show this book to the mediators, and tell them you are following this process. Make sure they feel comfortable in supporting the No-Load Divorce process.

Expect to spend about $1,000 per couple on mediation fees. If you don't have a No-Load Divorce mediator, the average charge for mediation is from $75 to $200 an hour, and you'll probably need two to three sessions lasting from two to three hours each.

Mediation is part of the No-Load Divorce process because we believe a mediated settlement will be a stronger settlement. Mediation encourages both parties to have a say in reaching a mutual agreement. It is empowering for each spouse. Mediation thrives on open discussion. Our experience shows that mediated divorces are usually faster, less costly, and less likely to be brought back to court and reopened.

▶ *Negotiating Tip #3*

PREPARE A SCRIPT.

As you prepare for your negotiating sessions, write out a script containing your arguments for whatever you want from the negotiations. Lawyers will often do a mock trial before they go to court. This is a dress rehearsal to refine their arguments and to help anticipate reactions. You can do the same. Perhaps you can ask a trusted friend to play your spouse and react to your requests.

Dress rehearsals give you lines to use during the real negotiating sessions. They will expose you to and help you plan for emotions that will surface during potentially volatile sessions. Practice your dress rehearsals only once or twice. Practicing more will make you more wedded to your script and less able to think on your feet.

›› Selecting Financial Advisers

A divorce involves as many financial decisions as it does emotional and legal decisions. That's why we'll devote the next two chapters largely to the financial issues.

In all cases—and especially in cases involving children and large assets—we recommend financial planning assistance. There are many long-lasting decisions involving financial matters during a divorce. We recommend that you use financial advisers affiliated with the No-Load Divorce network. They can be located on our Web site.

If a financial adviser affiliated with the No-Load Divorce network is not available in your area, we suggest the following guidelines in selecting a financial adviser:

► Make sure the financial adviser is licensed and has the proper qualifications to enact the transactions you will need.

► You want a professional who has proven experience in handling asset division for divorcing couples. Get references and check them.

► Make sure the financial adviser has the expertise or arrangements with other professionals to cover alimony calculations, child support calculations, business valuations, pension division, and tax implications. He or she should have affiliations with CPAs who are experienced in tax law (unless you already have a CPA with such qualifications).

›› Picking Your Two No-Load Divorce Lawyers

We recommend that you use No-Load Divorce lawyers. They can be located on our Web site. No Load Divorce lawyers are trained in the No-Load Divorce process and are committed to it. They have signed an agreement to avoid litigation and work toward an equitable settlement at a fair cost.

We know it will take time to recruit divorce lawyers across the United States who agree to meet our standards of practice. Therefore, on the next page we list 10 principles that apply to No-Load Divorce lawyers. If you cannot locate a No-Load Divorce lawyer, ask the lawyer you select to take the "pledge."

We recommend that each spouse secure his or her own legal representation. Each of you should have an opinion from your own attorney that the proposed agreement is equitable. Ethically, an attorney can only represent one party. Some divorcing couples select one attorney for both of them, but that attorney can only represent one of the spouses. In effect, the other spouse has no representation. Since our goal is to have the divorcing couple reach an agreement that lasts, we know each party must feel sure that their interests were taken into account during the divorce process.

›› NO-LOAD DIVORCE LAWYERS PLEDGE

As a No-Load Divorce lawyer, I adhere to these 10 principles:

1. I believe in the respectful approach of a No-Load Divorce and will operate in accordance with No-Load principles, given that you (the client) have made that decision as well.

2. I do not charge for the initial screening interview. You have a right to meet me and see if there is a fit before paying.

3. I provide you detailed information on how I charge and bill, including how I treat telephone and travel time, so that there are no surprises. I will give you an estimate of what the total charges will be. My goal is to help you obtain a divorce and at the same time minimize charges. [If you use a No-Load Divorce lawyer in our network, there will be a set fee. You'll have an outline of the hours the lawyer will work on the case, including hours set aside for appearances in court.]

4. I will be the lawyer reviewing and finalizing the No-Load Divorce agreement. I will not have an assistant or partner do the work.

5. I believe in and encourage mediation so that No-Load Divorce couples can work out most, if not all, issues between them.

6. Where there is dispute, I seek compromise and resolution, rather than to inflame emotions and mistrust. My focus is on an equitable solution that does not take advantage of either party.

7. I will return your calls in a reasonable time.

8. I will speak in simple terms and respect your unfamiliarity with legal jargon.

9. I will make sure that you understand the legal process and timetables, so that you understand where you are in the process at any given time.

10. I have sufficient knowledge of the state's divorce laws and experience in representing people going through divorce, in both negotiation and litigation. I know the habits and preferences and prior rulings of judges and referees in the family law area, and these judges and referees are familiar with me. I am familiar with the guidelines for child support and alimony and will share them with you.

SIGNATURE

DATE

Finding an attorney who is a good match for your needs and communication style is difficult. We think the best sources for finding an attorney (apart from our Web site) are referrals from friends, co-workers, or counselors. Local bar associations have referral phone lines. You can also look in the Yellow Pages under "Attorneys" and then under "Divorce." Remember, an attorney listed in the phone book doesn't necessarily follow the No-Load Divorce process.

Choosing an attorney can be difficult, and you may inadvertently select the wrong one the first time. Remember, the attorney is working for you. You are the boss. You have the right to fire your attorney and hire another one. The attorney you fire has the right to bill you for time spent on your case. He or she also has the professional obligation to turn your files over to the next attorney in an orderly and prompt manner. Changing attorneys does not affect the judge's opinion of you or your case. It also does not change the guidelines that will rule the outcome of your case.

Attorney fees are usually between $150 and $300 an hour. In most cases, you'll be asked to secure your lawyer with a retainer, or down payment. Then you will be billed monthly for time spent on your case. A No-Load Divorce lawyer will charge between $1,000 and $1,500 in attorney fees, mainly because you will have worked out most of the settlement issues before engaging the attorney's time. If you add about $1,000 for the mediation costs (per couple), the total legal and mediation bill should be between $3,000 and $4,000 ($1,000 for mediation plus $2,000 to $3,000 in total legal fees for the two lawyers).

›› Summary of the Structure of a No-Load Divorce

The chart on p. 69 illustrates the components you need to have in place as you go through the No-Load Divorce process. To summarize:

- ▶ For emotional support and clarification, both you and your spouse should be meeting regularly with someone who is trained to provide emotional support. This person could be your clergy, a counselor, or a marriage therapist. You may see this person as a couple and/or separately. We suggest that this support begins

▶ *Negotiating Tip #4*

ANTICIPATE MAKING CONCESSIONS.

You are going to have to make concessions during your divorce negotiations, so you might as well do it well. Here are five suggestions:

1. Make your smallest concession first with the hopes that you won't have to make bigger ones.

2. When you make your concession, look your spouse in the eye to emphasize that this is a serious loss for you.

3. After you make a concession, come back with a concession request of your own. Put it something like this: "Since I have shown good faith by making this concession, will you show yours by making a matching concession?" And then be prepared to suggest a concession of equal value to the one you made.

4. You can save face by reminding your spouse of a setback he or she experienced earlier in the negotiating session. "I guess I can give up X, since you gave up Y earlier."

5. Present what-ifs before you concede. Hypothetical proposals before you make final concessions do not commit you to a deal, and they may expose what is really important to your spouse. Once you understand that, you may be able to do a little trading or packaging, and the final concession may be more acceptable to you.

immediately. It should continue even after the divorce is complete and as you are adjusting to life as a single person.

▶ As a couple, you should retain a No-Load Divorce mediator with whom you both feel comfortable. You will be asking the mediator to help you reach agreement on custody, division of property, and other issues you have not negotiated on your own. As you reach various agreements, you will convert your No-Load Divorce worksheet into a draft for legal review. The worksheet is shown and explained in chapter 7.

▸ You need a financial adviser—preferably a financial adviser affiliated with the No-Load Divorce network—to help in the division of property. You may use one together, or each of you can hire your own. The financial adviser will help assess valuations, prepare cash-flow analyses, look at tax liabilities of various potential outcomes, help calculate child support, and recommend pension disposition. Based on your proposed agreement, they can prepare a financial profile for you. It will answer questions such as: When can I retire? How much do I need to save for retirement or college for my children? How will my financial picture look in 5 to 10 years? How much insurance do I need to carry?

▸ Each of you should retain your own lawyer, but make sure he or she is a No-Load Divorce lawyer. You should engage the lawyer when you are ready to file for divorce, so that you are able to consult as necessary. However, we encourage you to seek resolution of divorce issues by way of mediation before turning to lawyers.

▸ Start working on your worksheet by going to our Web site and using Starting Point. This service will take your data and information and then provide you with suggested property divisions, child support calculations, and alimony calculations. These divisions and calculations are based on the laws of your jurisdiction. This information, along with decisions you've made in completing the worksheet, is meant to serve as a starting point for your negotiations with each other, further guidance from your mediator, and input from your financial advisers. The result should be a proposed agreement you both endorse.

▸ Both lawyers should review this agreement draft. Once the lawyers are comfortable with it, and you both have signed it, the agreement becomes your final No-Load Divorce

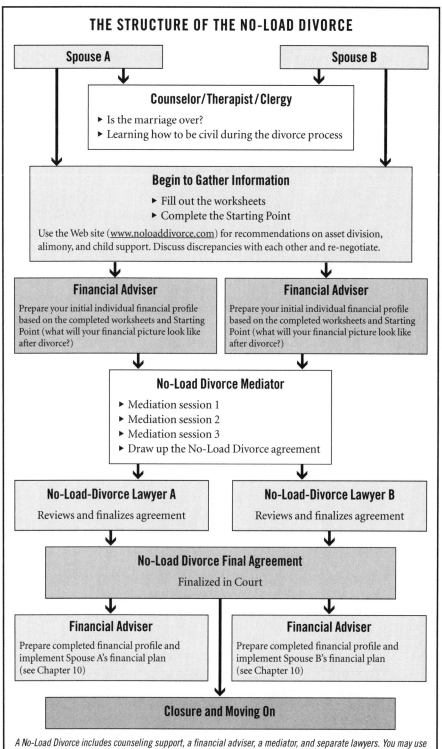

THE STRUCTURE OF THE NO-LOAD DIVORCE

Spouse A **Spouse B**

Counselor / Therapist / Clergy
- Is the marriage over?
- Learning how to be civil during the divorce process

Begin to Gather Information
- Fill out the worksheets
- Complete the Starting Point

Use the Web site (www.noloaddivorce.com) for recommendations on asset division, alimony, and child support. Discuss discrepancies with each other and re-negotiate.

Financial Adviser
Prepare your initial individual financial profile based on the completed worksheets and Starting Point (what will your financial picture look like after divorce?)

Financial Adviser
Prepare your initial individual financial profile based on the completed worksheets and Starting Point (what will your financial picture look like after divorce?)

No-Load Divorce Mediator
- Mediation session 1
- Mediation session 2
- Mediation session 3
- Draw up the No-Load Divorce agreement

No-Load-Divorce Lawyer A
Reviews and finalizes agreement

No-Load-Divorce Lawyer B
Reviews and finalizes agreement

No-Load Divorce Final Agreement
Finalized in Court

Financial Adviser
Prepare completed financial profile and implement Spouse A's financial plan (see Chapter 10)

Financial Adviser
Prepare completed financial profile and implement Spouse B's financial plan (see Chapter 10)

Closure and Moving On

A No-Load Divorce includes counseling support, a financial adviser, a mediator, and separate lawyers. You may use the same or separate financial advisers.

agreement. It can be submitted to the court as part of your divorce settlement.

▶ You both may appear at the final court hearing and disposition. Or the spouse who filed for divorce may appear without the other spouse. If both spouses have signed the agreement, the judge will approve the agreement and divorce as an order of the court, and the divorce will be final.

▶ After the court finalizes your agreement, your financial adviser will help you implement your individual financial plan. This includes changing the ownership of assets (including retirement plans), changing beneficiaries on insurance policies, up-

---

▶ *Negotiating Tip #5*

CLOSE THE DEAL, BUT DON'T RUSH THROUGH CLOSURE.

Closing the deal in divorce negotiations involves letting go of an issue, which may not be easy for you or your spouse. However, you can make closing easier by following these tips:

▶ Don't use the term *final offer* loosely. If this is indeed your final offer, then another proposal should not be made. Your body language and actions should confirm that you are finished.

▶ If your spouse is hesitant about closing a deal, emphasize what each of you has gained and the common ground you have unearthed during negotiations.

▶ Avoid sudden leaps forward, which can make your spouse nervous. Even though you are near closing, move deliberately.

▶ There may be some second-guessing from your spouse about earlier concessions. Hold fast to your main objectives, but have a few small concessions you can "throw in" at the last minute. Keep in mind an old saying: "It is better to sell the wool than the sheep."

dating or establishing estate plans, as well as dealing with other important financial issues.

›› Setting a Timetable

In a No-Load-Divorce, the two divorcing spouses have made a pledge to respect each other's pacing. We understand that the natural feelings of anger, resentment, hurt, and fear may cause you to rush forward, get through the divorce, and go your separate ways. However, we know of no one who, once divorced, felt that the time used to process feelings and explore settlement alternatives was wasted. Time allows for more certainty from both parties about the agreement. There seems to be a direct correlation between the time it takes to get divorced and the permanence of the agreement. Of course, there are exceptions; bitter parties can produce a drawn-out battle, and even after the divorce, they still want to fight. But they are exceptions, and most people look back on their divorce and appreciate the fact that a divorce takes time.

As we've said, the time from start to finish depends on whether there are children involved and how complex the assets are. The rule of thumb is that a divorce takes 3 to 18 months. Usually, the shorter the process, the lower the cost. With the understanding that all divorces are different, we suggest this timetable for a No-Load Divorce:

- ▶ Three months to cool off and sort out feelings, relying on help from counselors and clergy.
- ▶ Three months to work through the agreement with the mediator, the financial adviser, and the lawyers.
- ▶ One month to go through the final hearing and divorce.
- ▶ Six months of additional individual counseling and financial advice as you implement the agreement and begin new routines and a new life.

›› Taking the No-Load Divorce Pledge

You have the support pieces in place to begin the process of establishing the agreement. We'll go into that process in detail in the next two chapters.

All that is left is for you and your divorcing spouse to do in this chapter is take what we call the No-Load Divorce pledge.

This pledge is a verbal agreement expressed openly to each other. It may seem corny, but the act of saying it out loud to each other forms a commitment that will assist you as you both go through the process.

Like all pledges, this one is just words. But believe us, if you and your spouse can say these seven simple sentences to yourselves and to each other, the effect will be powerful and hugely beneficial to your future and to the future of your children.

›› THE NO-LOAD DIVORCE PLEDGE

I recognize that it is our mutual decision to end this marriage. The decision was made after much discussion and careful consideration by both of us. As we undertake the divorce, I promise open communications, honesty, and mutual respect. I want our decisions about our children to be in their best interests and our actions to protect their hearts and minds. I want our decisions about our property and our other financial assets to be fair and equitable. If we disagree, I promise to do so with respect and without verbal or emotional abuse. I understand that we both seek the same goal of a divorce agreement that is mutually acceptable and arrived at in a manner and time we both want.

You are now ready to begin crafting your No-Load Divorce agreement.

CHAPTER 5

The No-Load Road to Splitting Assets

The first time Don divided assets during a divorce, it was no big deal. "My wife and I had no real asset accumulation," recalls Don. The second time around, however, it was a big deal, costing Don $17,000 in legal fees.

Don pauses when he describes his second marriage. "It was difficult," he says. If you press him about the marriage, however, he will open up and use such words as "chaos," "turmoil," and "crazy." Don and Pam tried to blend families; he had three children from his first marriage, and she had one. This second marriage lasted nine years, during which Don and Pam separated twice. They were in counseling every year of the marriage, using six therapists.

Don was fighting through chemical dependency, and Pam, according to Don, had a "ton of issues. She got pregnant in high school and married the father of her child. Her father was a judge, who was verbally and physically abusive to her. Her mother was depressed and later committed suicide."

Don says Pam's mood changes were rapid and inappropriate. Angry outbursts were common, as were impulsive, self-damaging acts. "It was frightening," says Don, recalling his life with Pam.

"It got to the point, obviously, that my overall health and well-being were at risk. I knew that if I were to try to keep fixing this crazy situation, I would have a heart attack from the stress, and that my work and my parenting would suffer for years. So, the kindest thing I could do for her and me was to leave the marriage. I knew there would be financial consequences, but it was far better than suffering any more."

>› Both Hire Expensive Lawyers

Pam and Don's divorce was a real donnybrook, with expensive lawyers on both sides. Even though settlement guidelines were well defined for most issues, they wrangled over nearly every detail of retirement assets, the 401(k), the house, the cars, and on down the line. "I spent $17,000 in attorney fees, partly because she kept battling on issues that were non-issues," says Don. "Or she would agree to something but then not sign the documents."

After months of this, Don sensed that the divorce was moving too slowly. So he opted for a different strategy. He decided to pick his spots to fight. He would continue to stand up for what was his with the big items (house, 401 (k), and pension plan) but not get drawn into silly battles over inconsequential assets. "The furniture, she got it all," says Don. "I decided not to quibble over the cost of used furniture—or the outdoor grill or canoe or camping gear or whatever. Those things can easily be replaced. I saw immediately that fighting over the small stuff was just another opportunity for her to drag this thing out."

By coming to this realization, Don, to his credit, was able to seize the opportunity to show maturity and magnanimity. By rising above the fighting, he was able to separate himself—who he was and who he would be after the divorce—from what is ultimately the minutia of a divorce. When the divorce was finished, he could say that he liked himself and the way he handled the splitting of assets.

"Too often, people choose to become victims while they are trying to hurt their spouse in a divorce," he says. "They hurt themselves emotionally and financially, maybe because they feel guilty about the divorce. But after a while, I just wanted what was equitable. I didn't want to take advantage of her in the settlement. I wanted to let go of the pettiness and dispense with the emotional tug-of-war."

›› Take the No-Load Road

Don was not able to benefit from the No-Load Divorce process. However, once he saw how needlessly expensive his divorce was becoming, Don decided that he, at least, would take the high road, the No-Load road. As a result, he prevented an already expensive—financially, emotionally, and physically—divorce from becoming even more expensive.

The word we would like to highlight in Don's episode is *maturity*. We understand that when it comes to splitting assets, it is easy to become immature. The "Mine!" mentality gets mixed in with the anger and bitterness that are bound to surface in a divorce. Yet, rising above these emotions when splitting assets will not only lessen the costs of your divorce, but it will also make you feel better about yourself.

In this chapter we'll advise you on how to go about splitting assets in a civilized and productive way. This is a preparatory chapter for Chapter 7, which contains the No-Load Divorce worksheet. The worksheet helps you inventory your assets and begin to make decisions about how to split them. Completing the worksheet with your spouse—with the help of Starting Point on our Web site and members of your No-Load Divorce team—helps you face the reality of your financial and custody situation and then make difficult decisions. In most cases, you will have to live with these decisions the rest of your life.

As you continue to divide assets, you, like Don, may realize that there is more to a divorce than the minutia of dividing a pile of possessions into "his" and "her" lists. To coin a phrase, dividing assets does not build character, it *reveals* it. What we want this process to reveal is the nicer, fairer you. We want you to be a person who can give away that barbeque grill if that is slowing you down from becoming what you want to be in your new life. Therefore, in this chapter we will offer information that will help you:

- ▸ Envision your new life
- ▸ Focus on essentials of your agreement
- ▸ Reach fair financial decisions
- ▸ Tackle nuts-and-bolts issues concerning asset ownership and beneficiaries
- ▸ Prepare yourself for finality.

No doubt about it, this is tough sledding. But you are making good progress. Couples who have come this far tell us that just beginning the process of completing the worksheet has made the divorce seem more real. Their separate lives have begun to take form. Some of these couples, perhaps like you and your spouse, have not been able to agree on how to split assets. Nevertheless, they look at the worksheet and feel they have taken a huge step forward in ending their marriage. Just as important, they feel they have "traction," that now—finally—they are getting somewhere with this divorce. We hope you feel the same way.

That said, let's look at ways we can help you come to agreement as you divide assets.

›› Start by Envisioning Your New Life

Many divorced people appear to start new lives. Yet inside, they still feel emotionally tied to their old life. They can't fully envision themselves after the divorce. Unless you can truly picture a new life for yourself, you won't have a clear idea of the goals you are moving toward. You won't know how to divide your assets in a way that supports your new life. Your vision will always be behind you, not ahead.

We immediately think of our friend Tina. She was married to Chuck for 20 years. They met in high school, fell in love, never dated others, and got married during college. Tina and Chuck had two boys, but neither Tina nor Chuck seemed happy with their life together. They were sarcastic toward each other. They argued in front of their children and friends. Yet, for years they seemed resigned to this sad fate.

Finally, Chuck could not stand it any longer. He took up with another woman and filed for divorce. Tina assumed custody of the boys. She had plenty of education and degrees, but she couldn't seem to find an occupation that satisfied her. She relied on Chuck's large salary as a commercial real estate broker.

Their negotiations over assets and custody were bitter and never-ending. In fact, those same arguments have resurfaced periodically during the 15 years since the divorce. By outward appearances, though, Tina has successfully found her separate life. She has her own home, a new and successful career as an interior designer, financial independence, new friends, and a strong relationship with her boys, who are now adults.

However, whenever Tina talks about Chuck, she is still angry and disparaging. In short, even though Tina appears to have moved on in outward ways, inside she is still in a sense "married" to Chuck. She has not fully envisioned a new life for herself. This dwelling in the past has made for rocky negotiations over money and the children, both during and after the divorce.

Our point is this: Spend time envisioning your new life and keep that picture in mind as you divide assets. Make decisions that move you *for-*

ward in life, not decisions that hold you back, tied to the person you were in your marriage. We call this "getting to an endgame."

›› Getting to an Endgame

Many couples can't easily imagine what that endgame, and then their new life, will be. They have been married so long that they often don't have separate friends. One or the other may have handled all of the cooking, car maintenance, or household investments and bill paying.

Their first reaction to divorce usually is, "Now, who can I find who will do these things my ex-spouse used to do?" It is a matter of seek and ye shall find, right? Couples who ask this question will likely be answered with a new life much like the old one, but with a new partner.

Your new life does not have to be a carbon copy of the old. Since you are going to go through this painful divorce, why not use this time of self-examination to reassess whom you want to be—as well as whom you want to be *with*? It sounds like an overwhelming task, but here are some suggestions:

- Talk with people who have changed their lives. These may be friends, acquaintances, or someone you meet in a divorce support group.

- Make a list of traits that describe your current life. For each trait, write in a journal about whether you want to keep this aspect of your life—or change it.

- Start a new activity or hobby that is just for you. It might be something you always wanted to do but put off. Record in your journal how you handle the anxiety of trying this new activity. Make lists of what you like and don't like about this change in your life.

- Read autobiographies about people who inspire you. They may offer insight into how they faced similar challenges.

- Do things by yourself, like going to a movie, eating at a restaurant, or taking a weekend trip. When you were married, you and your spouse seldom were apart and probably feared the loneliness after a divorce. Find out now if the saying is true: The biggest fear is fear itself. You may even relish the joys of solitude! Successful time by yourself will strengthen your confidence and open you to envisioning more options in your new life.

We want to emphasize that envisioning a new life is not only good for your future but will also serve you now as you split assets. Here are three examples of how a new vision may help as you negotiate the division of your property:

A fresh start

Some women (and a few men) have devoted their married lives entirely to raising children and keeping their homes running smoothly. As they face divorce, however, often their children are more independent, if not on their own. These parents may decide now is a time to try something new.

How does this affect splitting of assets? Instead of negotiating for ownership of the family home, these "fresh start" parents may prefer to sell it, free up equity, and purchase a townhouse with fewer upkeep demands. In their new vision of themselves, they want flexibility and time to try new things.

A healing and predictable life

Many people who get divorced are simply not ready for too much change. What they want is time to heal. They envision a life of financial stability and predictability, with time to move slowly. This wish for stability may be particularly appealing to someone who has been in a chaotic marriage, as Don was.

How does this play out in asset division? These people decide they want the current house and furniture and enough money to live in relative security for a few years. They may be willing to give up some retirement security for the near-term benefits of stability.

A time of liberation

We have known people who use exciting travels as a response to their divorce. They feel liberated and may want to share this feeling with their children. They decide they want to take their children scuba diving or on a Himalayan trek. They have a passion to live *now*. So in the divorce agreement, they give up large chunks of retirement savings or the house for ready cash and a custody arrangement that lets them share their liberation with their children.

We could present countless other examples, but you get the idea. The point of envisioning your future is this: The best way to begin asset-splitting negotiations is to know what you value and where you want your life to be in the next few years. Clarifying the new life you want after the divorce will greatly facilitate discussions about the division of assets during the divorce.

›› Focus on Four Essentials

Splitting assets can easily become complicated. There can be so many assets to divide and emotions to sort out. You can become worn down by the process and find yourself going in circles or into silly cul-de-sacs, like who gets the electric toothbrush. Our advice is don't sweat the small stuff. Keep your focus on these four essential goals:

1. Economic security of both parties

Most important, never forget the need for economic security for you and your spouse. You may have strong feelings about your spouse, but when you look back on this divorce with some detachment, you don't want to regret a decision that ultimately left your spouse—and your children—in dire straits. You both need financial means because both of you will likely have similar expenses to cover with less income. You must recognize too that the courts want a fair and equitable settlement that promises each of you the highest possible degree of economic security.

There is usually a transition period as you and your spouse move toward this economic security. If one of you has chosen to raise the children and not work outside the home during your marriage, your transition time will involve paying bills with one income while one spouse raises the children. Or both you and your spouse may have to come up with resources to pay for day care, children's education expenses, and the cost of training and education if one of you plans to prepare for or re-enter the workforce.

Although your marriage is probably ending in a few months, your financial obligations to each other do not end as quickly. You and your spouse may be "economically married" (sharing income and assets) for many years to come, even after the divorce. Accept that.

Economic security derives from:

- Enough income to cover current expenses
- Life insurance to cover the possibility of death before the end of the obligation
- Protection from catastrophic loss
- A rainy-day fund
- Growing retirement savings
- A sound education savings plan for your children.

We rank these aspects of economic security in this order for a reason. If you have limited economic resources, you'll want to take care of needs at the top of the list. If your assets are larger, then work your way down the list until the money or assets are fully divided. Your financial adviser should help you with this division or at least consult with you so you can be sure these things are taken care of in the proper order.

2. Continuity for the children

We'll go into this in greater detail in the next chapter. For now, remember that a fair economic settlement must provide for a reasonably consistent environment for the children as they go from one parent to the other. If there are large economic discrepancies in the parents' environments, the children may feel manipulated by the "rich" parent or pity for the "poor" one. Children crave continuity and fairness.

3. A lasting plan

Economic disparity in the agreement often leads to other problems that come back to bite the spouse who thinks he or she "made out like a bandit." The spouse who feels economically cheated may take it out on the children, use them as a weapon, or take the ex-spouse back to court to ask for additional economic relief. A fair plan is likely to be a more lasting plan, allowing you to get on with your new life.

4. A sense of financial fairness

It is almost a cliché that every divorcing spouse says he or she didn't get a fair deal. Sometimes it is true, but quite often, when all is said and done, most people who have experienced a successful divorce will conclude that their settlement was generally fair.

How do you know if your agreement is financially fair? You can get an indication by using these two simple tests:

Does it pass the test of time?
If the decisions look fair today, let them sit a few weeks. Then revisit them. Do the decisions still look fair? If so, they likely are. This period is also a great time to meet with your financial adviser to make sure the current settlement contains investment diversity and holds up well against future inflation.

Does it pass the "smell" test?
Does your mediator think the division is fair? Mediators have years of experience assessing the fairness of asset division. They can sniff out an unfair split, and they also have samples of fair divisions used by their many past clients. Does your division of assets pass the mediator's "smell" test?

Our advice in splitting assets is don't get distracted by deciding such matters as who should have the toaster. That's the small stuff that pales in comparison to the four essentials of a financial agreement: economic security, continuity for the children, a lasting plan, and financial fairness. Keep your focus on what is essential.

›› The Nuts and Bolts of Asset Ownership and Beneficiaries

Here we speak from experience in saying that these issues can be complex, and you need help from a financial adviser. We can give an overview of the key questions you and your financial adviser need to cover:

How do you pay your bills?

If possible, you should stick to the status quo. In other words, continue to pay bills out of your joint checking and savings accounts, and keep track of these expenditures. We recommend that you not establish separate checking and savings accounts until after the divorce. In the meantime, both of you should have access to the joint accounts and be up front about the use of the money.

How do you manage current debt and avoid new debt?

Once you decide there is going to be a divorce, you need to make an agreement that no more debt will be incurred. Meanwhile, you must manage your current debt. It won't go away by itself. You both need to stay current on debt payments and your mortgage. As part of your settlement, you will decide who owns the debt once you are divorced. Typically, debt is transferred with the asset it is attached to, such as with homes, boats, and automobiles. Consumer debt, however, is usually split at the time of divorce.

What should you do with the home?

You may spend a great deal of time answering this question. The house can provide stability to you and the children. The house also represents the past and is filled with memories—some of which you may want to forget. Decisions regarding the house depend on your income and cash flow, as well as the age of your children. A house builds equity, and it may already have equity. Remember, however, whoever gets the house also must pay the mortgage, homeowner's insurance, real estate taxes, and maintenance and repair costs. (In divorce, the house is looked at as an asset with a net worth. The mortgage and related expenses come with it.)

What about health insurance?

If your coverage was through your spouse's employer, it might be continued for 18 to 36 months after your divorce. Your settlement should address who will pay the premium. If you need to switch coverage from your spouse's employer to yours, the change is usually allowable as a "change in family circumstances." Usually the spouse who has the higher income will pay his or her own health insurance costs and the children's. (Health insurance for the other spouse usually is paid by that spouse.) If income between spouses is similar, both parents will bear the cost. If either of you or your children will not have access to health insurance as a result of the divorce, your financial adviser should be able to help you find a policy.

What about life insurance?

The amount and kind of life insurance that are best for you depend on your income, your spouse's income, your children's needs, your custody arrangement, and other factors. Whole, universal, and variable life insurance policies build cash value. Term insurance policies do not accumulate cash values. All you are paying for is the insurance costs. Therefore, they are less expensive. You or your spouse already may have one or more of these policies.

The issues concerning life insurance are many. Generally, if one of you has an insurance policy, you need to decide who owns the policy, who is the beneficiary, and who will make the premium payments. If a policy has cash value, it should be considered an asset. You should also decide if you are providing adequate life insurance in case you die and your ex-spouse raises the children. You should spell out these kinds of details in your agreement. Consult with your financial adviser to make the decisions that are best for you.

What about disability insurance?

If you do not have disability insurance, you need it now. Why? You can no longer depend on the other spouse to cover your income needs when you are out of work due to a disability. Your financial adviser can help you find a policy. Some employers provide policies as well. Most policies cover 60 percent of your current salary. Premiums vary and are more expensive if the waiting period for benefits is shorter.

›› LIFE INSURANCE TO COVER CHILD SUPPORT

One of the most important needs in divorce is for the parents to have a life insurance policy that protects the children from loss of child support if the paying parent should die. In this case, we feel strongly that you should get as much insurance for as little cost as possible. This is a temporary need that generally goes away when the children reach 18. We think temporary, or term, insurance is the appropriate solution.

Let's look at a few examples. In both cases, let's assume the father is 42 years old and is paying $1,000 a month child support. In the first example, there is one child, age 2. The father is liable for 12 months x 16 years at $1,000 a month, or $192,000. A term insurance policy at this face amount would cost between $240 and $335 a year. The policy should have a level premium guaranteed for 20 years and be from a reputable insurance company.

In the second example, suppose there are two children, ages 2 and 4. The father is liable for $360,000 over the course of the obligation. A term insurance policy at this face amount would cost between $354 and $480 a year.

In both instances, the parent responsible for child support should pay the premium. Both parents should receive a copy of the premium notice so that the parent receiving the child support can be assured that the premium is being paid. The beneficiary of the life insurance policy should be a trust that pays the child support on a monthly basis. A trustee could be a sibling of either of you. Money remaining in the trust after the child or children become adults could be used for things such as college funding and weddings, or distributed directly to the children, until the trust assets are depleted.

To calculate the proper amount of life insurance to cover your child support obligations, go to our Web site. This is an essential calculation and is part of the Starting Point. You can shop for term rates on the site, where you will find competitive rates from reputable companies.

Who owns the pension?

You own part of any pension, Individual Retirement Account (IRA), or 401(k) retirement plan owned by your soon-to-be ex-spouse. The amount you own is generally one-half of the amount invested and earned during your marriage. This works both ways if you and your spouse have retirement plans. The process of transferring your portion to you is called a QDRO, a qualified domestic relations order. You can roll over that transferred portion into an individual IRA or retirement plan in order to keep sheltering your portion from taxes.

The main advantages of an IRA versus a 401(k) or retirement plan are broader investment choices. There also may be more tax benefits to beneficiaries. IRAs also offer more control over distributions. Continuity planning for heirs may be made easier by continuing to work with your financial adviser. When the QDRO is being distributed to you, you can take a portion out and pay taxes only on that amount, with no penalty for early withdrawal. This penalty-free withdrawal option can be done only once at the time of distribution. Consult with your financial adviser before making these decisions. A wrong decision could result in a stiff IRS penalty and could be potentially disastrous to your long-term financial security.

Can I get my ex-spouse's Social Security?

The laws, rules, and regulations that determine what Social Security payments you qualify for are complex, especially if you have been divorced. Rather than deal with the rules here, we urge you to visit your local Social Security office or log on to www.ssa.gov for more information. In many cases, you will be better off claiming your ex-spouses benefits rather than your own.

Should we change any ownership of assets or beneficiaries of assets?

Yes! Make changes according to the No-Load Divorce agreement you reach. Make these changes *after* you draw up the agreement, sign it (you and your spouse must sign), and include it in the court order granting your divorce. The judge must sign this court order. Most financial institutions and employers can supply the forms you must complete and sign to transfer ownership of assets or rename beneficiaries. Debts (such as credit card accounts with outstanding balances) need to be retitled too. It is a relatively easy, but often overlooked, process. Be sure to keep a list of changes you need to make, and then follow through. This can all be coordinated when you implement your personal financial plan with your financial adviser.

Tax issues

Here is the subject for another book! There are so many questions. Who claims the children as dependents? Should you file as a single head of household the year you are divorced? When your ex-spouse pays you money, is it a tax deduction to your ex-spouse and taxable income to you? Is child support taxable? Do you qualify for child-care tax credits? What about dependent-care reimbursement plans? Is any life insurance payout taxable? What about a cash value loan? If after the divorce one of you is in a lower tax bracket, is there an advantage to the other? These and other tax questions need the advice of your financial adviser and accountant.

›› Preparing for Finality

Suppose you have worked through the division of assets in a fair and equitable way. You have done your inventory, assigned values, split the assets, covered the debt, made sure ownership and beneficiary issues are in order, and made wise use of the tax law in preparing your financial settlement. Well done! You are nearing the end of your divorce, hopefully with the feeling that you are in control and are being fair.

You may also have another feeling. Many people have told us they experienced an "out-of-body" sensation while working through the specifics of their divorce. They seemed to be watching themselves from a once-removed vantage point at the far corner of the ceiling. We tell them that no, they were not in the Twilight Zone. More likely, this is the result of transitioning from the person you were in your marriage to the person you are becoming as you go through the divorce. This weird feeling is simply a way that you are preparing for change and coming to accept the finality of your divorce. So relax. It's normal (unless you hear Rod Serling call your name).

The final major step in the No-Load Divorce process is to agree on a custody arrangement. In chapter 6, we'll review some of the key custody issues. We'll also spend considerable time looking at how to focus on what is best for the children, and even on how to plan for their financial future. By the end of chapter 6, you'll have the information you need to make custody decisions.

When Divorce Really Hits Home: Custody, Child Support, and Alimony

Many divorcing people can remain at least somewhat detached and unmoved when discussing asset splitting, legal paperwork, and other details of divorce. But when they talk about custody and child support, the divorce really hits home. It hurts. It hurts because their heart aches for their little ones, who are confused and brave and wounded all at once.

For divorcing parents, the central and most important issue is caring for their children after the parents go their separate ways. Obviously, there are other issues involved, but often they don't really matter to parents—not compared to custody and child support.

We understand that you have a strong interest in doing the best you can for your children during and after the divorce. In this chapter we're going to cover issues and ideas related to custody, child support, and alimony. This will help you complete those portions of your No-Load Divorce worksheet.

This chapter will help you consider the child's perspective (What do children caught in divorce really want? What are their rights? How do they view what is going on?). It provides detailed information regarding custody, child support, and alimony. And it addresses how to deal with your children during and after the divorce.

This chapter is devoted to you and your children. We want to help you make rational decisions about your children's welfare—and your own—even though these issues can be confusing and extremely emotional.

›› One Child's Perspective

Joyce is now 23, a recent graduate of the University of Illinois in Urbana. Her parents divorced when she was 2 years old, and, as she describes the custody arrangement, "They pretty much split me right down the middle."

She was OK with this arrangement. After all, it was the only life she had ever known. Her parents hardly saw each other and therefore seldom fought. She had adjusted to their contrasting styles of parenting. Mom was strict, and Dad was laid-back. Mom was a vegetarian, and Dad had a weakness for sweets and junk food. Split custody did not affect school. No matter where she slept, she attended the same elementary school. Most of her school friends were also children of divorce.

The only negative aspect of bouncing back and forth between Mom and Dad was when they would whine to her about the other parent. "Actually, they would yell at me," Joyce recalls. "Mom would say something about Dad being so lax about food, and Dad would express his dislike for something Mom did. I didn't like being put in the middle, but I didn't say anything."

All things considered, though, Joyce was doing all right until fifth grade when her mother decided to move from Illinois to Colorado, in part to start a new career as a florist. The move was going to break the custody agreement. So her father took her mother to court.

"I remember Mom was at a neighbor's house when a car pulled up in front of our house," says Joyce. "Mom knew she was being served court papers, so she kind of hid at the neighbor's. I was there as well because I liked the neighbor's dogs. There was a knock on the door, and when we opened it, someone threw papers at Mom and said, 'You've been served.'

"Mom broke down crying, and I was confused. I was afraid of Mom being so upset, and I thought Dad was mean for doing this."

Dad won in court. Joyce would stay with Dad in Illinois, where she could maintain her current life, school friendships, and flute lessons. She would stay with Mom in Colorado in the summers. Mom and Dad tried to keep Joyce out of the court proceedings, but Joyce was forced to have an interview with what was then called a court-mandated child advocate.

"He wasn't a good child advocate," says Joyce, holding back tears. "He told me anything I said was confidential, and then asked me where I wanted to live—with Mom or Dad. I said with Dad, but I also said I didn't want to hurt Mom's feelings. I also said I didn't like Mom's boyfriends because they would fight. I did like the boyfriend she had then—he was the nicest one—because he would let me flush Mom's vegetarian food down the toilet.

"The child advocate then called Mom and her boyfriend into the room and told them everything I had said—everything. He broke our confidentiality agreement. Mom and her boyfriend were hurt. They cried and I cried, but no one said anything."

In the intervening years, Joyce and Mom talked about this pivotal incident a few times but not in much depth. Joyce was afraid of Mom's emotions. Joyce also sensed the strain when she would visit Mom. "She wouldn't have me there for a long time during the school year, and then I would come in the summer, and she would have to be a parent again," recalls Joyce. "A boyfriend would leave, or she would throw one out. She would get angry about little things, or we would battle over food. She would yell and get physical and say mean things about Dad. I was not happy when I was with her."

As Joyce grew up, she desperately held onto her love for Mom and began to understand Mom's struggles, especially with money. "She was making $6,000 a year then and could barely afford to feed herself, much less help me," says Joyce. "Dad was doing well, and he funded almost all of my college education. But he would get upset at her for having to pay for all of college. I listened to him complain about her for two years, and then finally I said, 'Stop! If you don't want to pay for it, fine. Or you can talk directly to Mom. But I don't want to be in the middle anymore, and I don't want to hear you complain.'"

Today, Joyce is as close to both Mom and Dad as she has ever been. She worries about them but is grateful that Mom's life is stabilizing. After having one date in high school and being very selective about men in college, Joyce is serious about a guy. Perhaps her fears about marriage are dissipating now that Dad has happily remarried. "It has been good for me to see how a real marriage works," she says.

In past chapters, we've described the benefits to adults able to go through divorce the No-Load way. As you can see by Joyce's story, the pain of divorce is especially felt by the children, too. Our hope is that No-Load Divorce will help minimize the pain for children of divorce.

›› What Children Really Want

Often, what children really want is that there be no divorce—and they will tell you exactly that, bless their hearts. But beyond this plea, they may not say right away what more they want in the divorce. They may be like Joyce and not say anything initially. It may be too painful to think about life after a divorce. They may think about it but have a difficult time picturing this life. Or they may be too angry to talk about it. This is natural. However, psychologists and family counselors say that in most cases children eventually reach a point where they can articulate their needs. It is then they admit that what they want is:

- ▶ *To know what is going on.* When it comes to a marriage, children can be like canaries in mine shafts—the first to show signs that something is wrong in their parent's marriage—in some cases sensing the danger even before the parents know. Children need to have their hunches confirmed. If you are getting a divorce, you need to tell them. Consult your therapist to learn what would be helpful to tell your children, depending on their ages.

- ▶ *To know they aren't to blame.* Children commonly believe they are the cause of a divorce. They may think, to the utmost dismay of their parents, that if they were better kids or at least better behaved, then Mommy and Daddy would not be getting a divorce. You must assure your children that the cause of the divorce has nothing to do with them. You and your spouse are getting divorced because you don't love each other any more, and you don't want to live together.

- ▶ *To know that you are not divorcing the children.* Children understandably fear a change of such magnitude as a divorce. They quickly figure out that divorce means a change in how often they can be with each parent. They need assurances that both parents will do everything in their power to be with the children as much as possible.

- ▶ *To be able to keep loving both parents.* Even though you may dislike the person you are divorcing, your children don't have this same dislike. They still love both parents, and divorce does not take away that love. Don't try to lobby the children to be for you and against the other parent. Let them have their own feelings and their own relationship with each of you.

- ▶ *To know it's OK that Mom's rules are different from Dad's.* We have seen parents fret about how their children will react to the different rules at Mom's home versus Dad's. Kids are amazingly adaptable, however, and can quickly adjust to leading different lives at the different homes. Some even find the differences fun.

▶ *To be immature.* That's right. Children, by definition, are immature. To be angry with a child for being immature is like being angry at a frog for being green. They just are. Accept that, like you, children will be moody, angry, irrational, defiant, or depressed as they go through the divorce. Children need you to be a positive role model, showing patience and tolerance toward them, your ex-spouse, and yourself.

As you make your custody decisions, remember this list of what children want. Remember also to avoid the temptation to use your children to hurt your spouse, even though you may be angry. By fighting for sole physical custody and keeping the children away from your spouse, you may think that you are getting back at him or her. But in most cases, you are hurting the children. You may also be hurting yourself because your children will come to resent you for keeping them from their other parent.

When negotiating custody, always keep in mind what your children want, which is basically to love and be with both parents as much as possible. We are not advocating that all physical custody cases be 50:50. What we are suggesting is there are many agreements that restrict children's access to one parent or the other. Usually, this restriction is done because of anger between parents, not because the children want it or because it is necessary to protect the children.

›› Custody

Remember the movie *The Money Pit?* It was a comedy about a couple that threw thousands of dollars into fixing a house that always needed one more thing to fix. Well, it can be the same with custody—only there is no comedy involved. Custody squabbles can be a money pit, especially when couples are quick to pull in their lawyers to fix their emotionally charged custody arrangement. Ask our friend Beth.

You may recall Beth's story from chapter 3. Beth shakes her head at the volatile feelings she had about custody. "I wanted to vilify my ex-husband," she recalls. "And I also wondered how I could be so stupid as to make children with this person whom I don't get along with."

Beth spent about $20,000 to get a divorce that included the custody agreement she so earnestly wanted. The agreement was that she had primary physical custody. The two children stayed with their father every other weekend and every Thursday evening from 4 to 8 P.M. Bad feelings between Beth and her ex about this agreement showed up in a number of ways, including punctuality. "He never did bring back the kids at 8 o'clock on Thursdays," says Beth. "He was late."

Also part of that agreement was a clause to reevaluate custody when the children reached age 10 or so. Recently, Beth and her ex did the reevaluation, which led to a disagreement. He wanted 50:50 custody, and Beth didn't.

With almost the same acrimony that they showed nearly a decade earlier, Beth and her ex went at it again, lawyers in tow. The result was 50:50 custody in the summer. However, the revised agreement stipulated that during the school year Beth had the children Mondays, Tuesdays, and Wednesdays, and her ex had them Thursdays, including overnight. Each of them had the kids every other weekend, and each had vacation times in the summer.

As you can see, the result was not that different from the initial agreement. Had this been a No-Load Divorce back in the early 1990s, Beth and her ex could have probably worked out a new agreement. But it wasn't a No-Load Divorce, and the emotional sore that developed between them with the divorce festered, leading to another $20,000 legal bill. All told, Beth has paid about $40,000 to lawyers. Her spouse paid a total of $15,000.

Looking back, Beth recognizes how over-the-top she was in revisiting the custody issue. "I had turned over to my lawyer 10 years of documentation of every bit of his outrageous behavior," she says. "This became a 25-page document that was part of my case. I wanted the court to see, 'God, look at how right I am!' But when we sued to try to recover court costs, the judge was outraged about this document. He said it was excessive and that the lawyer's time should not be used to produce such a paper. So I learned to just stick to the facts."

These are hard lessons for people like Beth to learn. Bill has been there, and he knows how painful and expensive custody battles can be—

come. However, our belief is that the more you know about custody and work cooperatively with your spouse to reach a fair settlement, the less hassle—and lower legal costs—you will have in your divorce and down the road.

So, let's take a closer look at custody. Custody is an umbrella term that covers:

- Legal custody

- Physical custody

- Visitation schedules

- Child support payments.

Custody refers to the living arrangements of the children: where they live and who is responsible for them. Custody involves the responsibility for children until they reach adult age, which in most cases is age 18.

›› Legal Custody

Legal custody refers to the right to make critical decisions about the children's upbringing, such as their medical care, religion, and schooling. In 20 states, custody is split into two types: physical and legal. Physical custody refers to where the children live and the responsibility of taking care of them. In states that don't distinguish between physical and legal custody, the term *custody* implies both types of responsibilities.

Legal custody may be sole or joint. Sole legal custody gives the authority to one parent. Joint legal custody, which most courts favor, requires both parents to agree on the above-mentioned key issues in the children's upbringing. Courts favor joint legal custody because they know both parents usually have a strong interest in these issues. Courts say children benefit from experiencing both parents' perspective.

However, in cases in which one parent may not be competent to make these upbringing decisions due to such circumstances as mental illness or absence, the court may award sole legal custody to the other parent.

Once legal custody is set, it is very difficult to change unless there are serious issues such as child abuse or neglect. The same is true with physical custody.

›› Physical Custody

Physical custody refers to where the children live and the responsibility of taking care of them. There are three types. Sole physical custody means the children live with one parent most of the time. The other parent typically has scheduled times to be with the children, and the arrangement is called visitation rights. Joint physical custody means the children live with each parent roughly half-time. Split physical custody refers to arrangements in which the children live full-time with one parent for part of the year, and full-time with the other parent for part of the year. Split physical custody also refers to arrangements in which some of the children live with one parent, and some live with the other.

In more than 35 states, courts expressly prefer joint physical custody if both parents are able and want to share child-rearing responsibilities. Joint physical custody requires that parents, regardless of their attitude toward each other, regularly discuss and agree on the details of parenting. Joint physical custody can be the most expensive form of custody because both parents must maintain households for the children. Parents must have duplicate bedrooms, furniture, toys, and other items. However, this form of custody allows the children to benefit from the influence of both parents. (Even if you have visitation, it's likely that you will want to have duplicate bedrooms, and so on.)

Joint physical custody works best if the parents live close to one another. This causes the least disruption in the children's lives. Children can maintain friendships and stay in the same school they have been attending.

Joint physical custody is one of the greatest gifts parents can give their children. Parents are putting their love for their children and concern for their children's welfare above personal feelings of anger or bitterness toward their ex-spouse.

›› Visitation Schedules

In cases in which physical custody is awarded to one parent, the other parent may receive visitation rights. Visitation rights may be "reasonable" or "fixed."

Reasonable visitation is largely at the discretion of the parent with sole physical custody. It only works if both parents trust each other, communicate well, and genuinely want the children to spend time with both parents.

In most cases, courts prefer fixed visitation, assigned at particular times of the week. Parents and children know the schedule and can make plans accordingly. Schedules vary from children having little contact to spending 40 percent of their time with the noncustodial parent. Again, the courts prefer that parents agree on the visitation schedule and then spell it out in their divorce agreement. The arrangement should be as specific as possible, stating:

- ▸ Day or days per week
- ▸ Pick-up and drop-off times
- ▸ Whether and when the children will stay overnight
- ▸ If the summer schedule is different
- ▸ Holiday and birthday schedules.

If possible, you should have a visitation schedule prepared for when you meet with your mediator.

Time spent with the children by the noncustodial parent can have a bearing on the amount of child support, depending on the state (see www.noloaddivorce.com). Visitation should not be used as a weapon against the noncustodial parent to extract larger child support payments.

›› Child Support Payments

Child support payments are monthly payments from the noncustodial parent to the custodial parent. They may be made in cases of joint custody, too. (In some cases in which the custodial parent is the primary wage earner, the noncustodial parent may not be required to make child support payments.) These payments are court ordered and meant to help maintain the health and welfare of the children.

A Census Bureau study found that noncustodial parents are more likely to make child support payments if they are employed and involved with the children. In the study, 95 percent of fathers made the payments when they were employed. One-third of unemployed fathers paid nothing. Ninety percent of fathers with joint custody paid child support regularly; 79 percent of fathers with visitation rights, and 44 percent of fathers with no visitation rights paid child support regularly.

Whenever possible, courts set up a system of payments so that the parents do not need to transfer the money directly. Ideally, the state collects from the paying parent's employer. The payments appear as a deduction on the paycheck of the parent making the child support payments. The state then makes the payments to the parent who is receiving them.

Each state has developed guidelines to calculate a range of child support to be paid, based on the parents' incomes. These guidelines can vary considerably from state to state. Some states allow some leeway in setting the actual amount.

In determining who pays child support, courts consider these factors:

- ▶ The financial needs of the children (food, clothing, shelter, health care, education, day care, and so on)
- ▶ The parents' income
- ▶ The amount of time the children spend with each parent
- ▶ The number of children.

While child support guidelines vary according to the state, they usually follow a detailed formula. The formula is available from your state department that handles child welfare issues. We can calculate child support for your situation if you complete the Starting Point on our Web site. We will send this calculation to you.

Some parents resent that they are sending money to their ex-spouse. In reality, parents have joint responsibility for providing for their children. To the parents who complain about making these payments, we offer this reminder: You would be paying the same amount or more for the children's welfare if you had remained married.

Child support payments may be renegotiated at any time. Either parent must petition the court for a modification if he or she thinks that the child's needs have changed or the parent's ability to pay has changed. Generally, support payments are made until the child reaches legal age, dies, or becomes self-sufficient, whichever comes first. Support payments are not meant to fulfill the total financial obligation of the paying parent to the children. The paying parent is also expected to cover other expenses when taking care of the children. These expenses could include food, clothes, entertainment, gifts for parties, transportation, and other needs.

Under federal law, child support payments are not tax-deductible for the paying parent. Nor are they taxable to the receiving parent. State tax treatment varies by state. Generally, the custodial parent receives the tax deduction for the dependent child.

We want to emphasize that in most cases, courts do not want to decide custody arrangements. Judges cannot know or understand all the details and issues of the case. They fear that any decision they make could cause bitterness and resentment that would, over time, come back to the children and adversely affect them. Therefore, courts prefer that parents come to an agreement on their own. One of the driving forces behind the No-Load Divorce is a belief that our process will encourage parents to openly discuss custody issues and reach an amicable agreement.

›› Alimony

In many divorce situations, one spouse, usually the one caring for the children, has not been in the workforce. Often the divorce causes that spouse to take a new job at a wage lower than the wage of the spouse who has been working all through the marriage. Alimony, sometimes called spousal maintenance or spousal support, is meant to compensate that newly working spouse for a discrepancy in earning power caused by the marriage. Alimony is a non-issue in divorce cases in which both parents are working and earning incomes that are roughly equivalent. Women are more likely than men to have sacrificed careers and career advancement for child rearing. When women get divorced and their income is not supplemented by alimony, they usually see a dramatic decline in their standard of living. Statistics bear this out. According to the National Center for Health Statistics, in the year 2000, the average drop in the standard of living for women after divorce was 45 percent.

Alimony is meant to prevent or minimize this drop. It takes the form of a cash payment made from the ex-spouse who is working or earning a higher wage to the other ex-spouse. Alimony can be paid as a lump sum or in a monthly amount.

In cases in which alimony is warranted, the amount depends on state and county laws, and is often negotiable. The amount also depends on the discrepancy of incomes, the age of the person receiving the alimony, health matters, the education of the recipient, and the length of the marriage. In all cases, one spouse must have the ability to pay, and the other must have a demonstrated need. We will calculate your probable alimony payment with Starting Point.

Federal tax laws stipulate that to receive credit for alimony payments, the person paying the alimony cannot be living with the person receiving the payment. Further, the alimony must:

- ▶ Be in cash (or check or money order)
- ▶ Be court ordered as a result of a separation or divorce (stipulated in the decree and stated in the separation or settlement agreement)
- ▶ Not be child support
- ▶ Be limited to the lifetime of the recipient. (In most cases, alimony is paid only for a certain number of months or years).

If these criteria are met, the alimony payments are tax-deductible for the payer and taxable income for the recipient.

Alimony may be discontinued after the recipient acquires training or education that leads to a higher paying job. In some cases, alimony is paid until the receiving spouse remarries. In all cases, it is based on the number of years the couple has been married. There are cases in which alimony is paid for as few as 12 to 36 months.

Alimony is meant as a bridge to help the receiving spouse become self-sufficient.

›› Dealing with Children During the Divorcing Process

Parents are often peppered with questions about divorce from their children. "What do we say?" parents ask us. They are at a loss because they don't know how much to divulge about this emotional issue or how to help their children.

Actually, parents who get questions are often the lucky ones. Many children internalize their stress and fear about divorce. They don't want to talk to either parent about this. Yet their behaviors change. Younger children may revert to earlier stages of development, hiding in their room, wetting the bed, or crawling into bed with Mom or Dad. Preteens may let their grades slip at school or spend lots of time at their friends' houses. Teenagers can turn to drugs, alcohol, or promiscuity. They hurt because of you, and they want to hurt you back.

If you are getting questions from your children, seize the opportunity to create an open dialogue about the divorce. Explore and validate their feelings, perhaps using the skills you learned from your therapist. At the same time, *do not* use the conversation as a chance to bash the other parent. That is a conversation stopper if ever there was one. (Use friends and counselors—not your children—to process your roller-coaster emotions.)

When the questions are especially tough to answer, tell yourself that this is dialogue and dialogue is good—much better than silence. Keep the dialogue going with your children, and look for opportunities to ask them questions and hear their answers. If the dialogue stops and the children start acting out (getting quiet, isolating, slamming doors, not doing homework), try to understand that they are responding to the divorce with actions because they don't have the communications skills to convert actions into words. Help them get back to words, even if those words are hard to hear and say.

Below are typical questions parents hear from their children—and answers you might consider. Answers vary according to your circumstances and depend on the age of the child. Keep in mind that in all cases honesty is the best policy. Try to give your answers using a reassuring tone.

- ▸ *Why are you getting divorced?* We don't love each other any more as we once did. We have had many conversations about our marriage and have thought a long time about this. It is a difficult decision. We love you and always will. That part will not change. We will both continue to raise you even though we'll live separately.

- ▸ *Do I have any say in how this gets worked out?* Yes. We want to know what you think about this. For the most part, though, this is a problem between your parents. So, we have to work it out. But we want to keep talking with you about how it affects you so that we can understand how to continue to be good parents to you.

- ▶ *What will happen to me?* You will live part of the time with one parent and part of the time with the other. We'll try to arrange this in such a way that moving back and forth will not be too disruptive. We will make sure that you have a place in each house that is your space.

- ▶ *How long will the divorce take?* We're working together to make decisions. We think the process may take about six months. We'll try to keep you posted, and we hope you'll ask when you're wondering.

- ▶ *Will we move?* We may stay here, or we may move. In either case, you will have your own room or space for all your things. We know that is important to you, and it is important to us.

- ▶ *Will I always be with my brothers and sisters?* Yes. For the most part you will be together, but there may be times when one of you will spend time with a different parent. We will always discuss this with you.

- ▶ *Will I stay in the same school?* Yes.

- ▶ *What do I tell my friends? What will they think of me?* You can talk about this with your friends. Many of them may have divorced parents and will understand. For better or worse, divorce happens in about one out of every two marriages. It is common, and your friends should think of you in the same way they always have. You are not getting divorced. Your parents are.

- ▶ *Will I have the money I need for school activities and movies?* Yes. If money gets tight as we adjust to our new living arrangements, we'll look at this issue again and solve it together.

›› Should Children Have Rights During the Divorcing Process?

During the divorcing period, children often assume they have few rights. Parents seem to have all the power. Your job during this time is to assure your children that they do have rights, and that you recognize those rights and want to support them.

What are the rights of children in a divorcing family? Children have:

- ▶ The right for love from both parents
- ▶ The right not to see parents fight
- ▶ The right to be able to talk to either parent whenever they want
- ▶ The right not to be a go-between, used by one parent to send messages to the other
- ▶ The right to know the status of the divorce as the process occurs.

You can give general answers. Any information is better than none. Providing no information will likely increase anxiety.

Children need to be reassured that this is a difficult time for everybody, but that the new life ahead of them will work itself out. They can always count on the love and support of both parents along the way. In chapter 9, we'll get into more detail about co-parenting once the divorce is final.

›› About Teenagers

If your children are teenagers when you seek a divorce, they may want greater say in the custody arrangement—and the courts often will back them. What if your teenage children have a strong preference to spend more or all their time with one parent over the other?

(Let's assume this is not a situation in which there is potential for child abuse or endangerment from one parent. Further, let's assume that you and your soon-to-be ex-spouse agree on joint legal and physical custody, and that the two of you can communicate reasonably well about the children.)

You can best accommodate your children's preference if you have negotiated a joint physical custody arrangement that gives your teenage children the flexibility to change the percentage of time they spend with each parent.

Say, then, that a son, while still wanting to see his mom from time to time, suddenly wants to spend full-time with his dad. If the child protested to the court, usually the court would not stop the custody change from happening. Knowing this, we think parents should discuss the decision with each other and with the child. The goal of the discussion is to make sure the decision is thought out and not a reaction to a single event. After this discussion, if the child insists on living primarily with one parent, the parents should try the arrangement and see how it works. Because the change is not court ordered, the child can (and often does) later change his mind and go back to shared custody. He may even try full-time with mom. Remember, he's a teenager.

If you have more than one teenage child, the children may decide they want to split up and spend full-time at different houses. Again, the court usually recognizes a teenager's right to do so. As a parent, the best thing you can do is keep communications open and let the teenager experiment. Because these changes may cause disruptions in your day-to-day life, you can set a limit to how frequently you will allow a change.

›› Making the Crucial Decisions

Ultimately, we can't tell you how you should make custody decisions, but we hope that the information in this chapter gives you realistic ideas of your options. We also hope our discussions about what kids really want helps you keep their ultimate health, safety, and welfare foremost in your mind. Divorce hurts, and a custody arrangement that is the result of poorly thought out decisions by parents will make the hurt worse. On the other hand, a good custody agreement is the foundation of healing for your children—and you.

CHAPTER 7

Time to Walk the Walk: The No-Load Divorce Agreement Worksheet

We are not going to sugarcoat the matter: This chapter will probably be difficult for you. In previous chapters, we have asked you to think about issues related to a divorce agreement. But talking about something and doing it are not the same. Sometimes as we "talk the talk" about divorce, we may hold out hope that a miracle will occur and we won't have to "walk the walk."

In this chapter, however, we help you walk, step by step, through the completion of a worksheet that will be the foundation of your divorce agreement. You will use this agreement worksheet in dealing with your mediator. In the next chapter, we'll discuss how to work with your mediator to resolve differences and draft your agreement. We will also cover how to review your draft agreement with your lawyers.

Doing this worksheet will save you money because you are collecting information and reaching agreements without the expense of doing so through an attorney.

In short, you are now at the point of making final and difficult decisions about custody and financial issues and putting them on paper. Under normal circumstances in a strong marriage, most of these decisions would be formidable. But now, as the divorce process takes its toll and leaves you increasingly hurt and shaken, these decisions are especially vexing. The what-ifs will really start to hit home, and you will understand in a new way that you face a personal crisis.

As you experience this crisis, try to remember two things. First, the Chinese word for crisis is composed of the characters meaning danger and opportunity. The danger part is easy to understand—and dwell on—during a divorce. But our hope is that you also comprehend that this is your opportunity to respectfully end a marriage and move on to a happier life. This is your chance, so make the most of it.

The second thing to remember is that facts and time can be your allies as you go through a divorce. Facts can help you make decisions, and in this chapter we have a worksheet that will assist you in pulling together facts and developing a sound No-Load Divorce agreement.

But even with all the facts gathered, decisions can still be tough. When this is the case, give yourself time. Consult your counselor for support, and check in with your mediator and financial adviser. If you act with due deliberation, you'll find clarity in what at first seemed like impossible choices. Be patient and you will make progress.

›› Hold Off on Contacting Lawyers

If you and your spouse have agreed to a No-Load Divorce, use your lawyer sparingly. Remember, the No-Load Divorce lawyer's primary role is not to help you *arrive* at an agreement. His or her primary role is to *review* your agreement and help you anchor the agreement to the law. Therefore, instead of calling a lawyer during the creation of every aspect of your agreement, we urge you to:

- ▶ Gather information about the guidelines that dictate a normal settlement in your geographic area. This information is available from your county social service agency—it may take some digging—or from our Web site.

- ▶ Bounce your thinking off friends who have had similar experiences.

- ▶ Consult with your mediator and financial adviser.

- ▶ Talk with your divorcing spouse.

You may be surprised at how manageable it is to discuss issues and make small, positive steps that will move the agreement forward. This success you experience in reaching accord before the final divorce will also spill over to your life after divorce, when you and your ex-spouse will need to communicate with each other about your children.

›› Now Use Starting Point

We have referred to Starting Point (our Web-based planning tool on www.noloaddivorce.com) several times in previous chapters, but now, as you work on the worksheet, you will find Starting Point to be a particularly helpful tool. Starting Point will help you split assets and make two important calculations that are difficult to do without help from a lawyer.

The first calculation is an estimated alimony payment, if appropriate. We tell you who should get it and approximately how much should be paid. The second is an estimated child support payment, if appropriate. Since each state's (or even county's) alimony and child support formulas and calculations may be different, determining these two amounts would be difficult on your own—but easy if you use our Starting Point plan.

Starting Point tells you:

- Guidelines for alimony in your area

- Guidelines for child support in your area

- Scenarios for splitting of assets. This information is essential for your financial adviser to show how this settlement affects current income needs, children's college education, retirement planning, and the purchase of a new home.

- Insurance needs (the life insurance needed to cover alimony and child support obligations should the paying parent die before the obligations are met).

You will be asked to insert information from Starting Point as you go through the worksheet. After you complete the worksheet, we'll help you begin to resolve differences through use of a mediator (covered in the next chapter).

›› Complete the Worksheet

It would be impossible to present a worksheet that covers all contingencies. However, our worksheet addresses the key elements you must negotiate in formulating your No-Load Divorce agreement.

The worksheet's nine sections cover the key elements of an agreement. Make copies of this worksheet (or download it from our Web site) and then start filling in the blanks. In some parts of the worksheet, we put a lot of information in a small area and were forced to use small type or limit space. To compensate, use additional blank pages as you need them or write information in the margins.

On the pages following the worksheet, you'll find tips and warnings for each section.

THE NO-LOAD DIVORCE AGREEMENT WORKSHEET

1. PERSONAL INFORMATION

Your name: _____
FIRST   MIDDLE   LAST

Your Social Security number: _____ DOB_____

Spouse's name: _____
FIRST   MIDDLE   LAST

Spouse's Social Security number: _____ DOB_____

Children's names, ages, school grade, school name:

	FIRST	MIDDLE	LAST	DOB	AGE	SEX	SS#	GRADE	SCHOOL
Child #1									
Child #2									
Child #3									
Child #4									
Child #5									

No-Load Divorce mediator information *(this section can be filled out later)*:

_____
FIRST NAME   LAST NAME   PHONE

_____
ADDRESS   ZIP

No-Load Divorce lawyer information *(this section can be filled out later)*:

_____
FIRST NAME   LAST NAME   PHONE

_____
ADDRESS   ZIP

Spouse's No-Load Divorce lawyer information:

_____

FIRST NAME   LAST NAME   PHONE

_____

ADDRESS   ZIP

Date of marriage: _____

DAY   MONTH   YEAR

Your place of employment: _____

NAME OF COMPANY   NO. OF YEARS

_____

FULL ADDRESS

Spouse's place of employment: _____

NAME OF COMPANY   NO. OF YEARS

_____

FULL ADDRESS

Your phone numbers: _____

HOME   OFFICE   FAX   CELL

Spouse's phone numbers:_____

HOME   OFFICE   FAX   CELL

Other personal information *(prenuptial agreements, children from a prior marriage, and custody issues from a prior marriage)*:

_____

_____

_____

_____

_____

_____

_____

2. INCOME OF BOTH SPOUSES

Include all income from all jobs. If your income varies month to month, average the last 12 months.

Your current monthly pre-tax salary or wage: $ _____

Your spouse's current monthly pre-tax salary or wage: $ _____
(if self-employed, net income after operating expenses)

Current value of monthly pension expected, based on years of service:

Spouse A receives: $_____   Spouse B receives: $_____

Other regular income: _____

SOURCE   MONTHLY AMOUNT

_____

_____

_____

_____

3. JOINT ASSETS

These are assets that you have accumulated *during* your marriage. Any values and debt should be verified with the institution by both spouses.

ITEM	OWNED BY YOU	OWNED BY SPOUSE	JOINTLY OWNED	MARKET VALUE	OUTSTANDING DEBT	NET VALUE	AMOUNT THAT GOES TO YOU	AMOUNT THAT GOES TO YOUR SPOUSE
		CHECK ONE						
Home*								
Work retirement plan								
Work retirement plan								
Work retirement plan								
Pension #1 Name:								
Pension #2 Name:								

ITEM	OWNED BY YOU	OWNED BY SPOUSE	JOINTLY OWNED	MARKET VALUE	OUTSTANDING DEBT	NET VALUE	AMOUNT THAT GOES TO YOU	AMOUNT THAT GOES TO YOUR SPOUSE
		CHECK ONE						
Pension #3 Name:								
Pension #4 Name:								
IRA #1 Name:								
IRA #2 Name:								
IRA #3 Name:								
IRA #4 Name:								
IRA #5 Name:								
IRA #6 Name:								
Savings acct. #1 Name:								
Savings acct. #2 Name:								
Savings acct. #3 Name:								
Savings acct. #4 Name:								
CD #1 Name:								
CD #2 Name:								
CD #3 Name:								

ITEM	OWNED BY YOU	OWNED BY SPOUSE	JOINTLY OWNED	MARKET VALUE	OUTSTANDING DEBT	NET VALUE	AMOUNT THAT GOES TO YOU	AMOUNT THAT GOES TO YOUR SPOUSE
		CHECK ONE						
Bond #1 Name:								
Bond #2 Name:								
Bond #3 Name:								
Mutual fund #1 Name:								
Mutual fund #2 Name:								
Mutual fund #3 Name:								
Mutual fund #4 Name:								
Mutual fund #5 Name:								
Real estate other than home Name:								
Real estate other than home Name:								
Other assets Name:								
Other assets Name:								
Other assets Name:								
Other assets Name:								
TOTAL								

* Remember, the equity in your home is based on the market value less any outstanding debt such as mortgages or home equity loans.

SPECIAL ITEMS

These include furniture, jewelry, cameras, electronic equipment, art, washers, dryers, and other household items that have a value you can agree on and were not gifts to one party.

ITEM	WHAT IT IS WORTH	GOES TO SPOUSE A	GOES TO SPOUSE B
		CHECK ONE	
1.			
2.			
3.			
4.			
5.			
6.			
7.			
8.			
9.			
10.			

*Some older items may have little financial value but important emotional value. You will need to recognize this and negotiate accordingly.

4. BUSINESS OWNERSHIP

We will explain this issue later in the chapter. An outside appraiser can help establish the value of a business for purposes of determining the fair splitting of assets in divorce.

5. SEPARATE PROPERTY

This refers to property you or your spouse owned prior to your marriage. Generally, this property will not become joint assets. In other words, ownership will revert to the person who owned the property prior to your marriage.

ITEM	OWNED BY	BECOMES THE PRPOERTY OF

6. DEBTS

Both of you may own debts jointly or separately. Please complete the form below. Exclude your home, cars, medical and school expenses, and health insurance, which are covered under "Section 7: Other Financial Obligations." Here you might list snowmobiles, boats, motorcycles, credit cards, and so on.

CREDIT CARD DEBTS

CARD NAME AND NUMBER	WHO OWNS CARD?	AMOUNT OWED	AMOUNT TO BE PAID BY YOU	AMOUNT TO BE PAID BY SPOUSE

YOUR OTHER DEBTS

ITEM	CREDITOR	AMOUNT OWED	AMOUNT TO BE PAID BY YOU	AMOUNT TO BE PAID BY SPOUSE

YOUR SPOUSE'S OTHER DEBTS

ITEM	CREDITOR	AMOUNT OWED	AMOUNT TO BE PAID BY YOU	AMOUNT TO BE PAID BY SPOUSE

YOUR OTHER JOINT DEBTS

ITEM	CREDITOR	AMOUNT OWED	AMOUNT TO BE PAID BY YOU	AMOUNT TO BE PAID BY SPOUSE

State income taxes owed _____

You will pay $ _____ Your spouse will pay $ _____

Federal income taxes owed _____

You will pay $ _____ Your spouse will pay $ _____

7. OTHER FINANCIAL OBLIGATIONS

SPECIAL MEDICAL EXPENSES:

PERSON	CONDITION	ESTIMATED MONTHLY TREATMENT COST

After the divorce, who will pay these costs?

You $ _____   Your spouse $ _____

SPECIAL EDUCATIONAL EXPENSES:

PERSON	SCHOOL	ESTIMATED MONTHLY EDUCATION COST

After the divorce, who will pay these costs?

You $ _____   Your spouse $ _____

HEALTH INSURANCE:

_____
NAME OF INSURER   POLICY NUMBER

Who covers you? _____   Monthly cost: _____

Who covers your spouse? _____   Monthly cost: _____

Who covers the children? _____   Monthly cost: _____

After the divorce, who will pay these costs?

You $ _____   Your spouse $ _____

LIFE INSURANCE *(remember, term insurance does not have cash value)*:

Policy #1

OWNER	INSURER POLICY TYPE	POLICY NUMBER	FACE AMOUNT	CASH VALUE

Annual premium $ _____

Who will pay premium? _____

Who will be beneficiary(ies)? _____

How will cash value, if any, be split? _____

You get $ _____ Your spouse gets $ _____

Policy #2

OWNER	INSURER POLICY TYPE	POLICY NUMBER	FACE AMOUNT	CASH VALUE

Annual premium $ _____

Who will pay premium? _____

Who will be beneficiary(ies)? _____

How will cash value, if any, be split? _____

You get $ _____ Your spouse gets $ _____

Policy #3

OWNER	INSURER POLICY TYPE	POLICY NUMBER	FACE AMOUNT	CASH VALUE

Annual premium $ _____

Who will pay premium? _____

Who will be beneficiary(ies)? _____

How will cash value, if any, be split? _____

You get $ _____ Your spouse gets $ _____

(Normally, if child support is paid, it should be protected by some form of life insurance. Competitive term rates can be obtained on www.noloaddivorce.com

HOUSING EXPENSES

(usually the person who owns the asset after the divorce will make the mortgage payments. The owner needs to have the income to cover this expense.)

Principal home address: _____

PRESENT VALUE	MORTGAGE BALANCE

TOTAL MONTHLY PAYMENT (PRINCIPAL, INTEREST, TAXES, INSURANCE)

Second home or apartment: _____

PRESENT VALUE	MORTGAGE BALANCE

TOTAL MONTHLY PAYMENT (PRINCIPAL, INTEREST, TAXES, INSURANCE)

After the divorce, who will pay these costs?
You $_____   Your spouse $ _____

We have agreed that _____ will continue to live in the current home.

TRANSPORTATION EXPENSES

	MAKE	MODEL	YEAR	CURRENT VALUE	AMOUNT OWED	MONTHLY PAYMENT
Auto #1						
Auto #2						

Who will own Auto #1: _____

Who will own Auto #2: _____

The owner of the vehicle should pay costs for that vehicle (including insurance costs) out of post-divorce income.

8. CUSTODY ISSUES FOR EACH CHILD

Remember, with joint legal custody, both parents will be custodians. With sole legal custody, one parent must be designated.

For _____, we have agreed to: ☐ Sole legal custody
       (NAME OF CHILD) ☐ Joint legal custody

Custodian: _____
       (FOR SOLE LEGAL CUSTODY)

For this same child, we have agreed to: ☐ Sole physical custody
      ☐ Joint physical custody

Custodian: _____
       (FOR SOLE PHYSICAL CUSTODY)

For _____, we have agreed to: ☐ Sole legal custody
       (NAME OF CHILD) ☐ Joint legal custody

Custodian: _____
       (FOR SOLE LEGAL CUSTODY)

For this same child, we have agreed to: ☐ Sole physical custody
      ☐ Joint physical custody

Custodian: _____
       (FOR SOLE PHYSICAL CUSTODY)

For _____, we have agreed to: ☐ Sole legal custody
       (NAME OF CHILD) ☐ Joint legal custody

Custodian: _____
       (FOR SOLE LEGAL CUSTODY)

For this same child, we have agreed to: ☐ Sole physical custody
      ☐ Joint physical custody

Custodian: _____
       (FOR SOLE PHYSICAL CUSTODY)

For _____, we have agreed to: ☐ Sole legal custody
       (NAME OF CHILD) ☐ Joint legal custody

Custodian: _____
       (FOR SOLE LEGAL CUSTODY)

For this same child, we have agreed to: ☐ Sole physical custody
      ☐ Joint physical custody

Custodian: _____
       (FOR SOLE PHYSICAL CUSTODY)

If you have selected sole physical custody:
Explain who would have custody (of each child; of all children) and what the visitation rights would be. Cover typical weeks, weekends, evenings, birthdays, holidays, summers, and vacations. We suggest you put this information on a 12-month calendar.

_____

_____

_____

_____

If you have selected shared physical custody:
Explain who would have custody over which periods of time. Cover typical weeks, weekends, evenings, birthdays, holidays, summers, and vacations.

_____

_____

_____

_____

Total days/year with mother: _____

Total days/year with father: _____

If you have selected split physical custody:
Split physical custody is when all the children don't live in the same residence at the same time. Explain which children would reside with which parent and when. Cover typical weeks, weekends, evenings, birthdays, holidays, summers, and vacations.

_____

_____

_____

_____

9. OTHER

List other issues and agreements that have not been covered by the sections above:

_____

_____

_____

_____

_____

_____

_____

_____

_____

_____

_____

_____

_____

_____

_____

_____

_____

_____

_____

_____

›› Explaining the Worksheet Sections

Let's look at each section of the worksheet and discuss issues, potential roadblocks, and ways to reach a solution.

›› 1. Personal Information

We start you out with a section that is easier to complete than the rest. We want you to experience progress immediately. Mostly, we're asking you to put down basic facts that you'll need as you move into your single lives.

Some personal information may or may not apply. For example, if either of you has been married prior to your current marriage, you should share past divorce settlements and decrees, as well as custody agreements for children you had in a previous marriage. Another key document is a prenuptial agreement (if you have one) for your current marriage. This agreement may dictate how you divide certain assets or assign ownership of items.

Although this personal information section is relatively easy to complete, expect to feel some strong emotions. Just by putting information on paper, you are taking another step in understanding what this divorce will mean to you. As you move to other sections of the worksheet, issues will become more complex. You will need support and time to fill out these sections in a careful and mutually respectful way.

›› 2. Income

Start by recording gross pay per month for both you and your spouse. If you are employed by a company and receive a regular paycheck, this is easy to identify. However, if you are self-employed or work on a commission, your monthly earnings will vary. In this case, average the monthly earnings over the past 12 months. Don't forget to subtract operating expenses.

If either of you receives an annual bonus, and that amount is predictable, factor the bonus into the monthly salary.

You or your spouse may have other regular income, such as rental income or payments from trust funds. Determine these as monthly amounts by dividing the annual payouts by 12.

›› 3. Joint Assets

In this section, we ask you to inventory assets and divide them equitably. You will probably want to involve your mediator in this process after you have completed the worksheet, because the final outcome depends in large part on whether you live in a community-property state or an equitable-distribution state.

Community-property states include Arizona, California, Idaho, Louisiana, Nevada, New Mexico, Texas, Washington, and Wisconsin. All other states, except Mississippi, are equitable-distribution states. Mississippi is a lone-title state, which is like a community-property state except you keep anything that has a title in your name.

In a community-property state, most joint assets are divided equally between the spouses (unless for some reason you and your spouse decide otherwise). In equitable-distribution states, property is divided according to the contribution of each spouse in gaining the asset. This type of division depends on many factors, including:

- How much money or effort each spouse put into the asset
- Incomes of each spouse
- How long you've been married
- Your debts and your spouse's debts
- Tax consequences.

Sometimes it is easy to attach a value to an asset. For example, the value of a retirement plan is its current balance. However, you need to assign value to many other assets. If you can't agree on the amount for an asset, hire an appraiser to assign value.

When dividing household or special items, first determine if only one of you wants certain items, such as a bowling ball. Then try to equitably divide the others. If you can't, consider holding the equivalent of a football player "draft." In other words, you each alternately pick an item from the overall list.

Answers for how things are handled in your state can be obtained from Starting Point and from your mediator.

›› 4. Business Ownership

We could write a separate book on how to value a business and divide its assets in a divorce. The subject is complicated because there are many factors involved. These factors include:

- ► Type of ownership
- ► Variety of assets, including non-monetary assets such as name reputation
- ► Liabilities
- ► Cash flow
- ► Potential growth
- ► Operation of the business after your divorce.

This last factor is relatively easy to resolve if one spouse runs the business now. But often, spouses jointly owned and operated the business. Now what?

There is nothing that says a divorced husband and wife cannot run a business together. However, if you want to separate from the business, as complicated as it is to untangle business-ownership issues, it is vitally important. Often a business represents more wealth than all other assets combined (cars, retirement accounts, houses, and so on).

Our most important tip in this section is this: Hire professionals, including a professional business appraiser, and if you and your spouse decide to sell, a professional agent to shop the business. Check the Yellow Pages to find professionals or ask friends who have sold a business. These professionals use a number of accounting methods. You may want to use several and average the calculated values.

If one of you owned the business before your marriage, its value to the marriage usually reflects what you and your spouse built during the marriage, not what was there before the marriage. Valuation is complicated by the ownership structure, whether there are other partners, and whether one of you wants to continue participating in the business. If one spouse wants to keep the business and the other doesn't, he or she sometimes pays off the other spouse with non-business assets or agrees to pay the spouse in installments.

Finally, there is the issue of taxes. You must complete the business buyout within a certain time period for the buyout to be considered part of the divorce settlement and therefore not taxable. Income received after that period is taxable. Your accountant can explain further.

›› 5. Separate Property

This is property you or your spouse owned before the marriage. It is also gifts or inheritances to one of you during the marriage, given by someone other than the spouse. In most divorce cases, this property goes to the spouse who originally owned it. In other words, what's mine is mine, and what's yours is yours.

›› 6. Debts

In simple terms, there are three types of debts:

1. Separate debt, assigned to one of you before the marriage
2. Joint debt, which you incurred as a married couple
3. Debts either of you incur if you separate but before you are legally divorced.

Paying these debts is important because it will affect your future credit ratings. That's why we suggest that divorcing couples close out any joint credit card accounts and open separate accounts. In most cases, this begins to separate the liability.

Ideally, you and your spouse will be able to divide assets in such a way that you can pay off your joint debt. If not, even after you are divorced, creditors will view the remaining debt as joint debt. When you pay off a debtor of a joint account, be sure to close that account.

Remember, state and federal income taxes that you owe are debts you must plan for.

›› 7. Other Financial Obligations

This is a vital part of the agreement because it deals with active financial obligations that are important to your living arrangements, health, financial protection, and means of transportation. In most cases, these obligations involve ongoing payments and have ongoing value. After you split up, both of you will still need coverage, but now for two households instead of one.

You will need to pay special medical and education expenses. How you pay these expenses depends on how you divide assets and decide on alimony and child support. Who gets the health insurance, and who pays the premiums? Normally, children's health insurance is paid by the person paying child support. The spouse's health insurance may be the spouse's obligation. As health care becomes more expensive, premiums may become a significant part of monthly expenses. Make sure you cover these issues in your final agreement. However, your future health care costs normally are your obligation after the divorce.

Life insurance is a separate and important issue. If your spouse dies after the divorce, you must raise your children alone and will need a replacement income for the one that will be lost. Also, current policies may have cash values. Who should have access to those cash values for purposes of a policy loan? Who should continue to pay the premiums? Make sure there is insurance to cover obligations of child support. You and your spouse need to decide how to handle all of these matters. One of your options is to liquidate the policy and split the cash value. However, the insured's "insurability" should be considered prior to liquidation.

Making these decisions is hard work. But give yourself time, gather facts, and seek the support you need to get through this.

›› 8. Custody Issues

In chapter 3, we covered the ground rules for custody. We touched on custody issues again in chapter 6. In this section, we are asking you to begin making decisions that we can only characterize as gut-wrenching and heartbreaking.

Keep in mind, however, that by taking the No-Load Divorce path, you and your spouse have declared that you want to find a solution that is in the best interest of all parties. You're talking with each other and seeking professional guidance. You are doing the best you can with a difficult situation. We're now asking you to commit decisions to paper, which takes the process to another level—especially with matters involving your children.

As we said in chapter 3, in most cases parents select joint legal custody, which means that they have equal say in the health, welfare, spiritual, and educational issues involving the child. The harder decision is over physical custody, which depends on the many factors we discussed in that chapter (age of children, employment situation of parents, ability of parents to communicate with each other, and so on). Once you have made the physical custody decision—whether it is joint or sole—you will face innumerable smaller decisions about how to handle the weekly routine and special occasions. These include:

▸ Is it better for children to go back and forth every few days or weekly?

▸ Should the children have one primary home or two?

▸ How can you share children's birthdays?

▸ What if you have special visitors (like grandparents) on days the children are to be with the other parent?

▸ What about switching time if one parent has important personal or business events?

There are no pat answers, and, therefore, you have to be creative. You'll need to balance your children's natural wish to see both parents as often as possible with a practical need for continuity and stability.

Your custody solutions may never seem to be perfect. However, you need to start making decisions. Most couples find that as their children get older, they need to re-negotiate the details of special days and even overall time distribution. So, keep in mind that these decisions will affect you and your children until your children become adults.

›› 9. Other

Even though you may have covered the bulk of property and custody issues, there are others that will come up. What do you do with dogs, cats, and goldfish? Who stores your children's video games? Who keeps family photos and videotapes? What do you do with your wedding album?! Deal with them in this section.

Making it through this worksheet is no simple task. You've done some hard work. As a result, you are well on your way to completing the No-Load Divorce — and ready to start mediation.

CHAPTER 8

Working Less with Your Lawyer and More with Your Mediator

Steadily making your way through the No-Load Divorce worksheet will build confidence. In the process, you'll begin to get your arms around what can appear to be an overwhelming divorce process. You may find you can make more decisions than you thought. You'll see that making decisions is both empowering and calming.

However, the worksheet will likely help you identify issues and details that you and your spouse cannot agree on. What is the next step in the No-Load Divorce process? Mediation, not lawyers.

>> Learn from Jessica

If you learn one thing from us, please learn this: If you have a disagreement on the worksheet, don't rush to your lawyers. At this point in the book, we are sure this advice won't come as a surprise to you. But it bears repeating, because too many divorcing couples make the mistake of quickly calling their divorce attorneys and turning matters over to lawyers.

Jessica went straight to her lawyer, and just as quickly she was heading for a costly, crash-landing divorce and an escalation of hard feelings between her and Grant, her husband. But then, using common sense and determined not to lose control of the divorce process to lawyers, she and Grant managed to pull the divorce out of this nosedive and work things out without getting whacked by huge legal bills. Here is their story.

Jessica and Grant had been married for five years, but she knew it was a mistake from the start. "I just didn't listen to myself when we eloped," she says. "I was 15 years younger than Grant, and we had broken up three times before we got married.

"After we were married, I was in my 20s and started to change, but Grant stayed the same. He was not a bad person, and we thought alike when it came to money. But we had totally different interests, and we didn't communicate well. He was more sarcastic. I was more direct. I was a major football and golf widow, and he never saw much of me because I was a workaholic."

About two years ago, Jessica thought about a divorce. It occupied her mind for six months. However, she became hopeful about her marriage when their church organized a church-building project in Costa Rica. "I begged Grant to go so we could bond and kind of start over with our marriage. He refused but said I should make the trip. Something clicked inside me right then. I knew we were never going to want to do the same things. I realized he was a great roommate. But I didn't want a roommate; I wanted a husband."

When she was finally sure she wanted a divorce, Jessica did what she thought was right: She called a lawyer. Actually, she called several lawyers listed in the Yellow Pages. When she finally talked with one, she found herself being somewhat intimidated.

"It is hard enough when you go through something this painful anyway, but it was extra hard to have to deal with a lawyer on top of it all," she says. "You get scared because you don't know what is going on. And I didn't know I had any choice in a divorce but to hire a lawyer."

Her lawyer charged $2,500 for 10 hours of service. What did he do for that amount of money? "I have no idea," says Jessica. She admits to being so distressed at the time that she didn't pay much attention. She had the sense that her simple divorce (no children and no major disagreements in splitting assets) shouldn't take 10 hours. "Each time he called or I called him, I had the feeling that, *cha-ching*, he was making money."

Jessica's lawyer advised her that she was entitled to one-third of Grant's 401(k). She had no interest in his retirement fund. "It was not my money, and I didn't want any part of it," she says. She had a job in medical sales and didn't need Grant's financial help.

Jessica bought out Grant's stake in their house. Her lawyer said she should demand that Grant pay for half of the real estate agent's fee if and when the house was sold. Grant was not wild about paying half of the agent's fee. In fact, he didn't like the turn of events since Jessica hired a lawyer. Jessica says, "He told me, 'He is your attorney, Jess, and he is not representing my best interests.' He said, 'I trust you but not him.'"

And so Grant, fighting fire with fire, hired his own attorney, and a relatively simple divorce became complicated—and expensive. Soon after learning about Grant's attorney, Jessica told Grant, "There is no reason we need to get lawyers if we can agree on these divorce issues."

Maturity and common sense prevailed. Jessica and Grant met to divide assets, including the house, savings accounts (minus legal fees), and the two cats. They went through the house room by room, listing the TV, VCR, couch, TV trays, and so on in either her column or his. Jessica typed the list, and they were done. "To say the process took a couple hours would be stretching it," says Jessica.

The wisdom of removing the lawyers from the process not only prevented an expensive escalation of tension, but it also paid dividends in Jessica's relationship with Grant after the divorce. Recently, she had a chance to go on a two-week vacation but needed someone to take care of the cats. "I knew the cats loved Grant, so I asked him," says Jessica. "He said, 'Sure, no problem.'"

We advise you to learn from Jessica's example. If you and your spouse have agreed to a No-Load Divorce, use your lawyer sparingly. Work out as many issues as possible between the two of you, and then allow your mediator to work his or her magic. Let's take another look at mediation and why it is a vital part of the No-Load Divorce process.

›› Mediation Is a Must

Mediation is the next step in the No-Load Divorce process. A good mediator is a vital part of your No-Load Divorce team.

Why? We believe that if you mediate instead of litigate, you'll reach a stronger settlement. Mediation is empowering for each spouse. It is an important part of completing the worksheet and developing the agreement. Your sessions with the mediator allow you and your spouse to meet face-to-face, hear each other firsthand, and avoid the possible third-party innuendos that can occur by speaking through lawyers. Our experience shows that mediated divorces are usually faster, less costly, and less likely to be brought back to court and reopened.

In chapter 4, we offered guidelines for selecting a mediator as part of your No-Load Divorce team. Now you and your spouse are ready to take your completed, or almost completed, worksheet to your first mediation session.

We recommend calling the mediator you have chosen and scheduling two three-hour sessions or three two-hour sessions, each two weeks apart. This will give each of you time to think about what has been discussed and consider alternatives. We recommend you bring your worksheets from chapter 7 to the sessions. You and the mediator can refer to Starting Point (www.noloaddivorce.com) to confirm divorce guidelines in your jurisdiction that apply to custody issues and property settlement.

Don't be surprised if your worksheet changes as you go through the mediation sessions. Undoubtedly, there will be areas with which you need the help of your No-Load Divorce mediator to reach understanding and consensus. Your mediator will help you make the progress necessary to reach a final agreement pending legal review.

Your goal is to use the mediator to resolve all outstanding issues and complete the worksheet. You and your mediator will then use the worksheet to draft an agreement. This agreement represents the culmination of your collaboration to develop a fair and equitable settlement that is under your control and shows respect for each party. You can change the agreement at any time before your final settlement is filed with the court. But if you followed the No-Load Divorce process, your draft agreement will probably require only minor legal revisions going forward.

Just as important as saving money, mediation could save your children the grief of watching their parents battle using lawyers. The pattern of civil communication that you and your spouse experience during mediation will carry over for years to come. This could save your children the agony of witnessing in their parents two bitter, antagonistic people, and it could save your children emotional scars that could last a lifetime.

›› Karen and Kyle

To give you a better understanding of what you can expect during your mediation sessions, let's take you through three mediation sessions involving a divorcing couple and a mediator. All three people, by the way, are familiar with No-Load Divorce and fully endorse the process.

The couple, let's call them Karen and Kyle, call the mediator, Sherm. Karen and Kyle have done a great job in completing the No-Load Divorce worksheet, but they have custody and spousal maintenance issues they cannot resolve. They agree on three two-hour sessions, and schedule them two weeks apart. Actually, Kyle wanted just two sessions, but Sherm helped Kyle see that in order to cover their disagreements thoroughly and without rushing, they should stick with three sessions.

Karen and Kyle also agree that they will talk about custody in the first session and about splitting assets and spousal maintenance in the second, and then review their agreement, which Sherm will draft, in the final session. Karen wanted to talk about spousal maintenance and asset splitting first, but Kyle didn't. Sherm listened to both sides and then suggested covering custody first. Karen agreed after Sherm said nailing down custody puts the interests of their two children, Kris and Kenny, above all else.

Session #1

Karen and Kyle express to Sherm that they both want to be active parents and that they share many parenting values. "So do I hear correctly that you trust each other in parenting your children?" asks Sherm.

"That's right," answers Karen.

"Correct," says Kyle.

"You two are fortunate," says Sherm. "Many couples who sit where you are sitting have absolutely no trust in each other as parents."

Karen and Kyle say that they do feel satisfied in that regard. They then spend the rest of the session reaching the following custody agreement: They will have joint legal custody. Karen will have physical custody. The children will reside with Karen, who will stay in the family home. Kyle will move into a second home and will have the kids every other weekend, Friday evening through Sunday evening, plus one evening during the school week. This evening varies according to Kyle's work travel schedule.

After Kyle and Karen work out this custody arrangement, Sherm senses that Kyle, who by nature is very quiet, is unsure about this agreement. "You don't seem comfortable with this, Kyle," says Sherm.

"Well, it's not much time with my kids," says Kyle.

"Oh, Kyle, it's more time than you spend with them now," says Karen. "You're always traveling."

Sherm quickly suggests that they give this agreement some thought. They can always make adjustments in a subsequent session. Karen and Kyle agree to this, and the session ends.

Session #2

Sherm has Karen and Kyle restate their custody agreement. He asks if they are comfortable with the solution, and they both say that they are. Sherm then suggests they move on to the asset-splitting issues and spousal maintenance.

After studying the worksheet, Sherm sees that Karen and Kyle have succeeded in doing most of the asset splitting themselves. However, they need help with dividing the house and Kyle's retirement plan. Sherm suggests that since Kyle's interest in the house and the value of his retirement plan are about equal, Karen should take the house and Kyle keep his 401(K). Kyle, who earns far more income as an accountant than Karen, a part-time interior decorator, will make spousal maintenance payments. This will help Karen make mortgage payments until she can work full-time. Between now and then, Karen will continue interior design course work and build up her clientele so that she can become full-time when her youngest is in school all day.

Sherm explains to Kyle that he must pay child support and spousal maintenance according to state and county guidelines. Kyle understands this because he has already looked up this information on Starting Point. Kyle agrees to pay child support until the youngest child is 18, and spousal maintenance until Karen has been working full-time for two years, or until their youngest enters third grade, whichever comes first. Karen and Kyle also agree that spousal maintenance will discontinue if Karen cohabits with another partner or marries.

Karen and Kyle have been doing good work during this session. They are relieved to listen to the mediator because they have been going round and round about these issues for weeks. They appreciate Sherm's creative solutions and tell him so. They also agree with this financial proposal—with the understanding that they can still make a change next session.

Sherm says Karen and Kyle have made great progress. He closes the session by saying he will begin drafting an agreement, which they can finish in the final session.

Session #3

Karen and Kyle have checked with friends, counselors, clergy, and a financial adviser about their mediated solutions and report to Sherm that they are comfortable with them. At least Karen is. Kyle says he's OK with everything except the custody arrangement. He still thinks he is not getting enough of his children's time. He wants to have the children Thursday evenings through Monday evenings every other week. Karen rolls her eyes and says, "Here we go again."

Sherm reminds Karen that a lasting agreement is one that all parties feel truly comfortable with. He adds that it is better that Kyle brings up his dissatisfaction now than two years from now, when he may go to court to request a change. Kyle says he has received written assurance from his boss that he will travel only on Tuesdays, Wednesdays, and Thursdays. Karen is impressed with this news and seems more open to a change in custody.

Sherm points out that Karen may welcome the change, which would allow her more time to devote to her interior design business. There is about a 20-minute back-and-forth discussion about this, and then Karen finally agrees to the change. It would allow Kyle the extra time he wants with the children, and Karen the extra time she needs to build her business.

They spend the remaining 45 minutes of the session completing and reviewing the draft agreement Sherm has composed. They agree that Kyle will take the draft to his lawyer for review and then to be shaped into a final agreement. This final agreement must pass inspection from Karen's lawyer before being submitted to the court.

They end the final session, and Karen and Kyle thank Sherm for "getting them over the hump" with their issues and for helping them avoid potentially extensive and expensive legal feuding that might have taken months to resolve and could have created more animosity.

From this example you begin to get the idea of what to expect from mediation sessions. You will have made a wise move in turning over your disagreements to a professional. Mediators are trained—even gifted—in helping people help themselves get to "yes."

›› THE JOYS OF MEDIATION

Mediators can be immensely valuable as you go through the process of splitting assets. So, we thought you would be interested in hearing about mediation from a mediator's point of view. We asked Minneapolis mediator Gary A. Weissman to let us be a fly on the wall as he counsels clients.

First, he tries to establish chemistry with his clients and their lawyers. He is trying to defuse the legal, adversarial atmosphere that is often present. "I ask the lawyers: 'What are the impediments to settlement? Are you doing your very best to remove these impediments?'" Usually, says Weissman, the lawyers and their clients are so set on digging in their heels and protecting their positions that they have a hard time imagining any other strategy. (That's why in a No-Load Divorce we don't bring in the lawyers until the agreement is completed.) So, he asks all parties to turn this matter upside down and search for ways to succeed.

Next, he listens as the couple tries to split assets. He offers advice, makes notes, and resists the temptation to fix their problems. He wants to empower them to fix their own problems. "I try to impart to them that this is a safe place, a room full of amniotic fluid so you can't stub your toe," says Weissman. And I try to steer them 180 degrees away from how all of us are socialized. We have been taught to go to some authority—Mom, Dad, the umpire, the boss, the judge—who will make the big decisions for us and fix whatever is wrong. But in mediation, I tell the couple that they can make the decisions. They will look to me during a disagreement, and I say, 'It doesn't do any good to convince me. In the end, the vote is going to be 2-0 and I don't get a vote. Convince the person across the table.'"

Weissman says mediators want the couple to take ownership of the agreement. It must, in the end, be *theirs*—not his or hers or the

The Joys of Mediation continued on next page

The Joys of Mediation continued from previous page

mediator's. "I want this to be a durable agreement," he says. "I don't want one of them to hold his or her nose, sign the agreement, and then mumble, 'Boy, I got hosed.' You see, if one person is unhappy with the agreement, he or she may try to sabotage it."

Sometimes, the couple tries to scream their way to solutions. Mediators must expect a certain amount of this, says Weissman, because it can be fruitful. "I had a colleague who talked about this couple who came in screaming, screamed for two hours, and left screaming. She assumed they would not come back because the mediator thought nothing was accomplished. But they came back for their appointment the next week. The mediator asked if the last session helped. 'Oh, yes,' they replied, 'up until now, we have only talked through our lawyers. That was the first time we talked to each other in a long time. We got some things off our chest, and now we are ready to get down to business.'"

Weissman says all mediators have their own style and set of tactics. He, for example, is less patient with screamers than his colleague. "After a while, I will ask, 'Am I being helpful? After all, you are paying me $250 per hour.' That stops them and then they say, 'You're right. This is dumb.'"

Weissman says a crucial part of his job is to help parties actually hear each other through all the emotions. "The couple will be fighting over something, and I'll offer to repeat what I heard the wife say. I do, and the husband will look at me like I was speaking Serbo-Croatian. So I try to aid in communications because communications affect perceptions, and perceptions affect options in the agreement."

One may wonder why mediators like their job. Who wants to listen to people scream and argue all day? "The joy and satisfaction of mediating a case successfully is geometrically greater than that of winning a trial," says Weissman. "When I win a trial—even if the opponent is a jerk—part of me feels bad when I win too good. Often, both parties are unhappy and have spent thousands of dollars on this trial, and for what?

The Joys of Mediation continued on next page

The Joys of Mediation continued from previous page

"With mediating a divorce, there is the challenge of unscrambling the egg. The couple comes to me after their lawyers have shown they cannot do it. So I am rather smug, I admit, when I can get them to agree to their absolute satisfaction—and I don't have absolute power. I have gotten them to fix it. About 25 to 35 percent of family law involves post-divorce matters. Somebody wants a second bite of the apple because he or she is moaning and groaning about the first agreement. But with most mediated cases, they don't come back for seconds. They understand that it was their gig. They did the hard work—not the lawyers or the judge. They feel empowered. They say, 'We did this!' And they understand that once they get into a groove of agreement, they can deepen that groove and make decisions on their own."

›› Review Your Draft Agreement with Your Financial Adviser

It is important you meet with your financial adviser and review your draft agreement because you want to make sure that you understand how the agreement affects:

- Your income once divorced
- Your assets
- Your children's college education
- Your retirement planning
- Where you will live
- Insurance coverage (protection for replacement of child support and alimony)
- Estate planning needs.

Remember that your financial adviser is an integral part of your team. Financial issues were reviewed in greater detail in chapter 5. As you prepare your worksheet, you may want to refer to that section of the book. Even small changes in the agreement may have a large impact on your financial future.

›› NOW Call Your Lawyers

Now you are now ready for legal review of your agreement. The rest of this chapter is about hiring and dealing with a lawyer, a step that can make or break your No-Load Divorce.

Good lawyers can be lifesavers at a critical time. They can get the job done for you in your divorce, but there is a price to pay. Sometimes the price is reasonable, and sometimes it is not. Our point with all of the steps of the No-Load Divorce—and especially with this step of hiring and dealing with lawyers—is *you* have the most control in keeping the price reasonable.

In this section, we will help you find a good No-Load Divorce lawyer and work smoothly with him or her.

›› Selecting a No-Load Divorce Lawyer

You can locate a No-Load divorce lawyer by visiting our Web site, www.noloaddivorce.com. Our lawyer locator offers profiles and contact information on No-Load Divorce lawyers who are nearby and familiar with local family court judges, your state's divorce laws and rules, and the generally accepted property and custody settlement guidelines.

Though selecting your divorce lawyer seems like an overwhelming task, it is well worth your efforts. Our lawyer locator should help you come up with a short list. Then you must interview a lawyer on your list, making sure the lawyer agrees to take our No-Load Divorce lawyer's pledge, presented in chapter 4. (Those listed on our site have taken the pledge.)

Make sure the lawyer is a good personal fit for you. A good fit may mean the lawyer:

- ▸ Is a good communicator and speaks "plain English"
- ▸ Is attentive to details
- ▸ Meets deadlines
- ▸ Returns your phone calls in a timely manner
- ▸ Is organized
- ▸ Keeps you updated on your case

- ▸ Is someone who puts you at ease
- ▸ Is not antagonistic to your spouse or to the opposite sex in general.

Lawyers usually offer a free consultation *before* you engage them. Use this time to evaluate whether there is a comfortable personality fit. Come to this session with questions (see p. 141). You could even ask a friend to come along and observe the interaction to help you evaluate whether the lawyer is right for you.

As we have stated previously, No Load Divorce lawyers are trained in the No-Load Divorce process and are committed to it. They have signed an agreement to avoid litigation and work toward an equitable settlement at a fair cost. They have also taken the No-Load Divorce lawyer's pledge.

We recommend that each spouse secure his or her own legal representation. One attorney can review the document, if you prefer, but we prefer that each of you have an opinion on the proposed agreement from your own attorney. Your attorney should determine that the proposed agreement is equitable. Ethically, an attorney can represent only one party.

Some divorcing couples select one attorney for both of them, but that attorney can only represent one of the spouses. In effect, the other spouse has no representation. Since our goal is to have the divorcing couple reach an agreement that lasts based on informed consent, we know each party must feel assured that their interests were taken into account during the divorce process and that one spouse did not dominate the process.

Beware of organizations that promote contentious divorces or promise you that they will advocate for either men's or women's rights. These firms often encourage a bitter and costly divorce by creating conflict in areas where you have strong beliefs.

With a No-Load Divorce, you know in advance that you will pay between $1,000 and $1,500 in attorney fees. The fee covers the lawyer's time to review and amend your agreement, prepare your court filing, and accompany you to the final hearing. The fee is reasonable because you and your divorcing spouse will have worked out most of the settlement issues before engaging the attorney's time.

›› Questions to Ask Prospective Lawyers

Remember, the job of your No-Load Divorce lawyer is to review your agreement and make sure it complies with your wishes and agreements that were negotiated during the mediation. It is not the job of the lawyer to start or rekindle a battle. Use the following questions, and more of your own, to interview each lawyer you are considering to handle your divorce, especially if you are approaching a lawyer unfamiliar with No-Load Divorce:

- ▶ What is the process that will get this divorce to settlement?

- ▶ How long do you expect the process to take?

- ▶ Are details of this process and timetable in written form?

- ▶ How many sessions will we need to review and finalize my agreement?

- ▶ What is my estimated cost? Following your initial consultation, have these details spelled out in a letter of engagement from the attorney to you. This can help you avoid an unpleasant situation after you begin using the attorney.

- ▶ What kinds of preparatory work can I do for our sessions? (If you've followed the No-Load Divorce process, your preparatory work is done in the form of your draft agreement.)

- ▶ How does your work complement the work of mediators?

- ▶ What is the process for terminating our lawyer–client relationship if it turns out that you and I don't work well together?

›› What Should Happen During the Legal Review?

A successful legal review of the draft No-Load Divorce agreement requires that all parties work together in a spirit of openness and fairness. During this process, there needs to be a mutual understanding that:

- ▶ Both spouses and both attorneys have access to the same information, and

- ▶ Both parties will make full disclosure of financial information.

This information should already be laid out in your proposed agreement.

Above all, the attorneys must understand that the divorcing spouses carefully completed the worksheet and created an agreement with support from their counselors/clergy, mediator, and financial advisers. Ideally, the attorneys' role is to *review* the worksheet and agreement and then shape it into legal form. Lawyers look for oversights or issues that seem unfair or out of balance with typical settlements. The attorneys will undoubtedly make recommendations, but it is understood that they are not involved in order to trash your efforts and dominate the proceedings. Instead, their work will improve the work you've already done. Here is what your lawyers should do:

Review the worksheet and agreement.

Each of your lawyers should review your worksheet and agreement to make sure the agreement is fair and typical. They'll note anything that seems biased.

"I ask my clients to think of a 36-inch yardstick when approaching settlement issues," says David Harrison, a divorce attorney in Rochester,

---

›› WHY YOU SHOULD AVOID LEGAL BATTLES

- ▶ Attorney fees can skyrocket into the tens of thousands of dollars.

- ▶ Your children will get pulled into the fight, leading to life-long emotional scars.

- ▶ A judge or court-appointed mediator who doesn't know you or your children will be forced to make decisions that affect all of you.

- ▶ Your battle becomes a matter of public record.

- ▶ Both parents ultimately will feel ripped off.

- ▶ Your ability to co-parent after the divorce will be difficult.

- ▶ The settlement has a much greater likelihood of being contested in the years to come, and you'll be back in court.

›› A SHORT COURSE IN DEALING WITH LAWYERS

- ▶ Understand your attorney is not your friend. Get appropriate emotional counseling.
- ▶ Don't let the attorney stir up emotions.
- ▶ Maintain communication with your spouse.
- ▶ Don't get hung up on small issues.
- ▶ Do as much of the legwork as possible in tracking down necessary information.
- ▶ Understand that divorce rules and guidelines are established and will dictate much of the outcome of your divorce.

Michigan. "Ideally, you want all disputes settled at the 18-inch mark, but often they do not settle there, for one reason or another. So, I advise clients to try to produce a settlement that is fair and *reasonable*. In some cases, it is worth it to fight for a more favorable deal, one in which you are moving 12 inches on the yardstick toward more fairness. But in most cases in which continuing to fight just moves you maybe 1 inch on the yardstick, I advise clients that this settlement is reasonable and not worth more fighting."

Make amendments.

At the start of the legal review, you, your spouse, and both attorneys should agree on a process for amending the resolutions reached in the agreement. If your attorney identifies important issues, it is good to have a process in place for seeking resolution. It may look something like this:

1. When one attorney identifies an issue that should be addressed, the attorney discusses it with his or her client first. Together they decide if they will present the issue to the other spouse and that spouse's attorney. If this is an issue that you and your spouse have negotiated and are comfortable with, move on and don't revisit it.

2. All parties agree to notify each other with lists of the outstanding issues prior to any face-to-face meetings. Advance notification ensures that no parties are blindsided.

3. After the notification, each spouse–lawyer team meets separately to brainstorm possible compromises or solutions.

›› DIVORCE FROM THE LAWYER'S PERSPECTIVE

Minneapolis attorney Carole M. Megarry has been practicing family law for 25 years. She has seen all kinds of divorces, everything from the most complex, contentious cases involving "off to the races" custody disputes and business valuations to the straightforward "Divorce 101 cases," as she puts it. "I can tell you real fast how these straightforward divorces will shape up," says Megarry. "There are just not a lot of ways to go."

Megarry says most of her cases are of the Divorce 101 sort. "Of the 30 to 40 divorce cases I'll handle each year, only one will be a train-wreck case," she says. "I find those cases—with the battle of the experts, a high degree of mistrust, and the lawyers having to double back to check everything—to be really rare."

The straightforward cases, says Megarry, are made even more straightforward—and less expensive—when clients take classes or workshops to prepare for the divorce and do as much of the information gathering as they can. To keep matters simple regarding money issues and divorce, Megarry likes to refer clients to financial planners, who help clients with the tax ramifications of their divorce and assist them as they get a fix on their post-divorce finances.

A common and costly mistake of clients and attorneys, says Megarry, is focusing exclusively on custody disputes, which "can take on a life of their own" and overshadow other issues that need to be addressed in a divorce settlement. She advises clients to make sure their lawyers do not let custody issues detract from the task of moving all settlement matters toward resolution in a timely fashion.

According to attorney David Harrison, from Rochester, Michi-

Divorce from the Lawyer's Perspective continued on next page

4. The two attorneys and the two spouses then meet as a four-some to resolve the differences, hopefully in one session. If both parties are in accord with all the sections of the agreement, you do not have to have this meeting.

Divorce from the Lawyer's Perspective continued from previous page

gan, another common mistake clients make regarding divorce attorneys is assuming they have tricks to magically solve disagreements. "I'm not that clever," he says. "What I try to do over time is convince the other party and his or her lawyer that I am trustworthy, that I want to be as fair as possible to both sides. It is in my client's best interest that no one takes advantage of the other, with one party walking away with a bitter loss. This situation festers and comes back to bite everyone involved. I want my client, and hopefully the spouse as well, to go away from the divorce in better shape than when they came to me."

For someone searching for a good attorney, Megarry offers this advice: "Good divorce lawyers have to have really good boundaries," she says. "I tell my clients that I am not a therapist, I have no training in therapy, and at $175 an hour you shouldn't try to use me as your therapist. I am here to help people make clear decisions about divorce.

"I take no pleasure in contentious divorces, in cranking this thing up and watching it burn. The real point is to start with a set of facts and bring the proceedings to resolution, conserving resources as much as possible. In many ways, divorce is all about damage control. I tell my clients that if everyone is unhappy about the settlement—one spouse looks as if he or she is about to have a heart attack and the other spouse is reaching for his or her Valium—then the settlement is probably fair.

"I am an agent of change. Divorce is a big change in a person's life, and I am here to help them through that change."

The actual process you agree on is less important than the fact that you, your spouse, and your attorneys establish a process of resolution that you agree to in advance and that facilitates resolution.

Shape the final agreement.

Once both lawyers have completed the review and you and your spouse have agreed on any outstanding issues, you and your spouse should agree on which attorney will use the agreement to produce the final settlement. If attorney A (usually representing the party who filed for the divorce) produces the final settlement, attorney B should review it.

Having an attorney produce the divorce agreement is essential. Attorneys can make sure the agreement says what you intended it to say. They can remove ambiguity or confusing statements that later could cause squabbles.

Submit the agreement to the court.

After both attorneys have approved the agreement, you and your spouse will sign the document. Then attorney A attaches the agreement to a "stipulation for divorce" and submits it to the court.

Attend the hearing.

Within a few weeks or months, the court holds a hearing. Usually the spouse who filed for divorce needs to be present with his or her attorney, attorney A. The other spouse and attorney B can be present as well, but often this is not required. The judge, seeing there is a settlement, grants the divorce according to the stipulation and issues a decree making the divorce final.

That's right. You are now divorced.

CHAPTER 9

Getting to the Positives of Single Parenting

Before delving into the No-Load Divorce approach to co-parenting, we would like you to pause for a bit of reflection. Imagine you are now divorced.

Even after the divorce is final, you will probably have trouble believing you are divorced—and single again. That's natural. It will take time to accept. But make no mistake, the divorce is done, and you are moving on with your life. You not only went through a divorce, but you did it sensibly, prudently, and respectfully. You and your ex-spouse may have had to learn new behaviors to do this, but what you learned will serve you well, not only as you maintain relationships with your ex and your children, but also as you begin new relationships.

So, you have literally and figuratively "turned the page" on divorce. You are starting a new chapter in your life, and for those of you who have children, co-parenting is one of the most immediate and important tasks you now face.

As you and your ex-spouse are setting up separate households, your children are also trying to adapt. They are learning what it is like to not see both parents at the same time, live in two separate homes with different rules, figure out how to maintain friends from two places, and keep track of their clothes and homework. What they want most is stability, predictability, and routine. These are qualities not easy to find in the early stages of divorce.

There are enough advice books on co-parenting to fill a small library, and we encourage you to read some of these books and also seek professional help. In addition, we will examine in this chapter many co-parenting issues from the perspective of No-Load Divorce parents who want to cooperate and put the children's needs first.

We divide this chapter into these sections:

- ▸ Dealing with the immediate change and impact of divorce on the children

- ▸ What children want from their now-divorced parents

- ▸ Keeping children out of the middle of parental differences

- ▸ Turning single parenting into a positive experience.

›› Dealing with the Immediate Change and Impact of Divorce on Children

Jason's parents divorced when he was 9 years old. Both remarried. He spent time in each household as he grew up. Last year Jason, now 49 years old, got a phone call that his father had died. "My first thought—even with my parents being divorced for 40 years—was that now, for sure, they won't get back together," he says.

Part of dealing with the immediate impact of divorce is dealing with the children's persistent but natural desire that, somehow, this wrong can be made right. A child's longing for a magical re-creation of the parent's marriage may never go away. At the same time, parents may long for some of the nicer—often idealized—remembrances of their former marriage. A friend of ours, Sally, tells us she is happy to be divorced and now remarried. But she still longs for something she will never again have: a family dinner where the children are doted on at the same time by their adoring parents. "It's not the same when one of the parents is a stepparent," she says. "It's nobody's fault. It's just not the same."

Divorce causes huge losses and wounds that never completely heal, in both children and parents. The pain is bad in the first weeks, months, and even years after the divorce. The applecart has been upset. Everyone is dealing with new routines and inconveniences, while longing for the stability of the past. In fact, the past often gets romanticized as better than it really was.

Given that, how can you as a parent help your children deal with the immediate changes of divorce?

Remember, your children didn't divorce their other parent.

You may be angry with your ex-spouse, but your children probably are not. Your children love both parents equally. Your new job—which may rub you the wrong way at first—is to be a guardian of your children's love for the other parent.

In practical terms, that means you cannot speak negatively about your ex-spouse in front of your children. Don't even use a negative tone or look. Your children are tuned in to your attitude, looking for the slightest insult or expression of disrespect. If children hear you blast your ex-spouse, *you* will suffer for it. Your children will hear your attack and will naturally feel obliged to defend the ex-spouse. You will have lost some of your children's loyalty and respect, and you will have caused them unnecessary emotional turmoil.

If you're mad at your ex-spouse, find a soundproof room, lock yourself in, and scream to your heart's content. Or have a session with your therapist or meet with a friend for coffee (but not too often—you could lose the friend). At all costs, try to keep your anger away from the children. Let them enjoy their natural love for both parents. This is especially necessary right after the divorce, when children feel most insecure and both parents are preoccupied and less available.

One of our clients has a 14-year-old daughter who has witnessed custody battles between her parents over the past 10 years. She told her mother that she couldn't wait to turn 18. "I want to get out of your house and out of Dad's house," she says. "I just want to get out of the middle of all of this tug-of-war."

Do your best to speak in neutral terms about your ex at all times, no matter how you feel about him or her.

Keep the lines of communications open.

Children feel all sorts of emotions about the divorce, but they often lack the language skills to express them. They will depend on you to help them identify and accept their feelings.

How can you help your children share their feelings? One way is with the telephone. Put a phone extension in the children's room and encourage them to call their other parent whenever they wish, in private. When sleeping at Mom's house, kids should feel there is absolutely nothing wrong with calling Dad just before bedtime for a phone "tuck-in." This access creates a feeling of inclusion and fairness that may free them up to more easily discuss matters with you without feeling disloyal to the other parent. Some parents buy their teenage children cell phones so the teens can call either parent at any time.

Another way to encourage expression of feelings is to set up regular, special times when your children meet with an adult friend or relative for confidential talks. Emphasize that anything the child discusses with that friend or relative is confidential—excepting revelations of abuse. Then back off. And get over your hurt ego knowing that your child might be more comfortable talking about the divorce with someone else rather than you. Our client Jean told us that when her brother divorced, she set up weekly breakfasts with her niece. The niece could talk about the divorce and co-parenting issues in a safe environment. Nothing was shared with the girl's father. The niece, now an adult, remembers those breakfasts as a special part of her childhood.

Finally, practice being an empathetic listener. When you are talking with your children, try to listen for their feelings. Don't be quick to react, give advice, or put words in their mouth. For example, if your child says, "Daddy was mean to me last night," don't fly off the handle and skewer Daddy. Ask neutral questions, like:

- ▸ "What happened?"
- ▸ "How did you feel?"
- ▸ "What would you have liked to say to Daddy?"

It's hard to appear neutral when you have strong emotions about Daddy, but you can do it. Your goal is not to "get" Daddy but to gain your child's trust in talking about the divorce. You want your children to feel safe in expressing their feelings. If you react with judgments, the children will clam up, and your opportunity for open communications will pass.

You'll find it just as hard to be neutral when your children take a crack at you. Suppose Johnny says, "Daddy lets us do that." Resist your natural reaction to defend your way. Explain in neutral terms that you and Daddy (or Mommy) have different rules. Explain why you have your rules, and then leave it at that.

Expect a transition period.

As you set up your new household, your children will need time to adapt to the change. Anything can happen in this transition period. Some children pretend to be unaffected. Others become unglued. Some react immediately. Others "crash" five years later. For every action there is an equal and opposite reaction—and divorce is a BIG action. Your children's reaction will come but not in any predictable way. How children react to a divorce can depend on their age, gender, position in the birth order, whether the parents live near each other or far apart, and many other factors.

So what can you do, given the unpredictability? First, keep the lines of communication open—between the children and you, and between the children and your ex-spouse. With open communication, you will know when your children are reacting to the divorce, and you will be able to help them with the reactions.

Second, create the kind of normal home life you had, or hoped to have had, when you were married. A predictable, routine home life is a rock for children reacting to divorce. There is no reason why you, as a single parent, cannot give them this. You can establish chore lists, have rules and expectations, and keep the day fairly structured with regular mealtimes and special fun times.

Rusty, another of our clients, says the transition time for his daughter to adjust to the divorce took years. He raised his daughter as a single parent, starting when she was three years old. He was patient and saw that the adjustment, hurt, anger, and scars emerged nearly every year as his daughter grew up. He also discovered different techniques to try to help her along the way.

"When she was little," Rusty says, "I created a voice for one of her dolls. At bedtime the doll would talk to my daughter about all the doll's problems growing up. The doll was funny and neurotic—or at least I thought so—but it touched on some real issues that my daughter was experiencing. The doll would ask my daughter for some advice, and this gave my daughter an opportunity to talk and gain confidence as well."

When his daughter was a teenager, Rusty used other techniques. He made sure she had lots of contact with his extended family so she wouldn't feel isolated. He encouraged her friendships with children from other divorced families.

"I knew I was doing the right thing when she began to push me away as a teenager," he says. "To me, that meant she was secure and had pretty good self-esteem. She wanted to do what all healthy teens do—separate from their parents and act confidently."

In college Rusty's daughter still had moments of emotional crisis stemming from the divorce. He encouraged her to seek a campus counselor, which she did. "I don't think the hurt of divorce ever goes entirely away," Rusty says. "So my goal all along was to create situations in which she would learn how to identify and share her emotions about the divorce. I wanted her to build confidence that she could do this without me, on her own, as she goes on and lives her life."

›› What Children Want from Their Now-Divorced Parents

Divorced parents do not have an easy road. They must provide their children with normal parenting (if there is such a thing). At the same time, they must help them cope with living in two households.

Children are trying to get back to normal, and normal is all new because you have turned their life on end by getting divorced. If the home life during the end of your marriage was strained, then there is a good chance your child's new, post-divorce life will improve. This is possible, perhaps probable, since presumably you will be happier, and your household will be free of the stress of a failing marriage. As much as your children did not want the divorce and will feel the divorce pain for years to come, they also do not want you or their other parent to be unhappy.

Beyond wanting their parents to be happy, children also want you to provide the following:

A return to order.

Their lives are topsy-turvy. They will be spending time in two different homes with new places to sleep, new ways to get to school, disruptions to access to their friends, and less immediate access to both parents. In the midst of this massive change, children crave stability, order, and routine. And you? You are adjusting to changes galore and find yourself distracted and distraught. Look for ways to insert structure in your children's life, and yours: regular mealtimes, bedtime stories, weekly trips to the ice cream shop, pancakes on the weekend, watching a video together at regular times, and so on.

Your attention.

As they try to adjust to the divorce, your children may cling to you or push you away. In either case, what they really *want* is your attention and assurance of your love. They want to know you don't blame them for the divorce and that you won't go away. As preoccupied as you are in adapting to your new life, be sure to be present for your children. Look for times you can spend together, whether it is during the drive to school or making dinner together. In this time together, avoid direct questions, which many children don't like. Find ways to connect and converse that are indirect. Talk about the latest sports star or movie star, what kids are wearing, or details about your day. Watch your attitude. Don't sound desperate or hopeless. Children want to feel that life, despite being so different, is still good.

Pleasant relations with the other parent.

You are not just any divorced parent. You are a No-Load Divorce parent. You have concluded your divorce with respect and finality, and you can now get on with respectful co-parenting. If any two people can learn to share information about the children and respect each other's different parenting styles, you two can. Your children want you to be friendly toward each other. If they sense discord, children may internalize it. Once festering inside the children, the discord can come out in a variety of behaviors—anything from depression to anger to psychosomatic illnesses.

A consistent standard of living.

Our friend Robyn and her ex, Tom, had different standards of living and parenting. "I was a graphics designer, and I probably made one-fourth Tom's income," says Robyn. But Robyn made sure she asked for what she needed in the divorce settlement and then lived within her means after the divorce. By doing so, she made sure that the difference in incomes made no difference in how their son, Brent, lived—no matter at which home he stayed.

If you have been true to the No-Load Divorce process, you and your ex-spouse have been diligent in adhering to the guidelines in your area so that your children can have a consistent standard of living between houses. Your children want fairness, and they want some semblance of order and sameness between their life at Mom's and their life at Dad's. If Dad has a fancy sports car, a boat, and a mansion, while Mom lives in an apartment and can barely afford to put food on the table, the children will see the difference. They may feel embarrassment at Mom's house and not want their friends to come by. Or they may be angry with Dad for not being fair. Mom might complain to the children, and they'll feel caught in the middle. Children want the differences between Mom's and Dad's homes to be as minimal as possible.

Privacy.

Children of divorce want a private relationship with each parent. They don't want to be asked too many questions about their life with the other parent. The children fear they are being interrogated and the information will be used against them or the other parent.

Here's an example of what happens all too often. It starts when Mom asks what the child did at Dad's home.

"We went to a movie."

"Which one?" Mom asks.

"*Godzilla Eats All the Children.*"

Mom picks up the phone and calls Dad. "So," Mom barks at Dad, "I heard you took our children to a violent movie. How dare you!"

Now Dad is angry with the child for telling, maybe even for failing to keep their special "secret." If the child didn't tell, Mom would be mad. How can the child win? No wonder children stop telling parents things.

Even though you will be curious about what happens in your ex's home, let your children have some privacy in their relationship with the other parent.

Emotional space during "switch" time.

One of the most difficult times for children is right after they "switch" from one parent's home to the other's. Each time this occurs, they must sort through all kinds of feelings. They immediately miss the parent they are leaving. They must get used to the rules at the other home. Their room is changing. Their toys and clothes are changing. The parent in the home they have come to is hungry to connect with them. It can be tense for children and parents alike. The parent must put the children's needs first by giving the children time to adjust. Usually it takes a full evening. "My kids used to get dropped off on a Monday night," our friend Phyllis says. "They'd either go watch TV or go into their rooms and put on their stereo headphones. They definitely wanted to be left alone. It took me a long time to accept this and not take it personally. I had to put aside my wrong assumption that the children didn't want to be with me. They just needed time. By morning, they were back at my place physically *and* emotionally."

A sense of family.

Children want and need contact with extended family. Encourage visits with their aunts, uncles, cousins, and grandparents on both sides. In Robyn's case, often Tom would not show up to pick up Brent on scheduled weekends. Because of the pain and neglect Brent was feeling in his relationship with his dad, it would have been easy for Robyn to stop Brent from seeing Tom and all of Tom's relatives. "But I decided that would have been really selfish and mean on my part," says Robyn. "There is no point in carrying my animosity forward. I did not want to be stuck in the past forever and then carry these feelings to my grave. And Tom's parents and relatives have thanked me because they wanted to be a part of Brent's life as well."

Grandparents can be a great sounding board and safe haven for your children. At Grandma and Grandpa's house, children can process the changes and emotions they are experiencing. In many cases, grandparents genuinely do not take sides during a divorce and continue to have good feelings toward the ex-spouse. Children sense this and feel safer sharing with their grandparents what life is like after the divorce. Experiences with extended family also helps children of divorce feel more normal because their friends who have non-divorced parents talk about times with their larger family. Then there is the practical matter of a child of divorce spending time with a grandparent because the parent is working or less available. The special bond that forms can be a lifelong comfort for the child, grandparents, and parents.

›› Keeping Children out of the Middle of Parental Differences

Numerous studies have shown that conflict between parents—divorced or not—is one of the biggest reasons children have difficulty in life. After a divorce, parents no longer live together, often don't like each other, and don't communicate well, and therefore they may resort to communicating through their children. This puts the children smack dab in the middle of conflict and increases the chance that these children will suffer now and for years to come.

It is easy to assume parents use their children as go-betweens because the parents are mean. But in most cases, that is a wrong assumption. Parents use their children as go-betweens because:

- They're angry and hurt
- They want to justify the divorce to the children
- They want the children to side with them
- They want to avoid talking with their ex-spouse
- They feel insecure about their children's loyalty.

The case can be made that you need to stop putting your children in the middle of *all* communications with your ex-spouse—even when the communication seems pleasant. Our adult friend Ken tells us how his father wanted to use Ken to "just say hello to your mother." This simple request used to send Ken into emotional turmoil. "Here my parents had been divorced for years," says Ken. "All my father had to do was pick up the phone and say hello to my mother if he wanted, but he would draw me in. It infuriated me. There were a million subtle messages in that request. Dad really was saying to me that he didn't bear any grudges, unlike my mother, who didn't want to ever talk to him again. Dad was trying to prove to me that he was the friendly, forgiving parent—the better parent and person. It felt like a slight to my mother.

"Besides, what am I, a carrier pigeon? Do I go to my mother and say hi from my father and then she says something that I'm supposed to carry back to him? All my father's remark did was make me never want to visit him again."

Outward conflict communicated through the children can be even more damaging. It can take many forms, such as:

- Mother sobbing and saying that she can't pay the bills while "your father cavorts around with his girlfriends"
- Dad making fun of "your mother's rules about every little thing that goes on in the house"
- Shouting over the phone while the children are within earshot
- Cold stares or harsh words when transferring the children from one home to the other.

So how do you handle conflict with your ex-spouse in an appropriate way? The No-Load Divorce way includes these six steps:

1. Do not react to or comment about your ex-spouse in front of your children.

If you want to scream in outrage, laugh in contempt, and jump up and down in disgust at the things your children tell you or that you observe, do whatever you can to avoid such reactions. Count to 10 before saying something. Draw on your serenity and willpower. Think about your children, not yourself. Know that they love the other parent—even with all his or her warts—and that love is essential to their healthy development. If you want to talk with your ex by phone, make sure you are out of earshot of the children, because they will be listening.

2. Learn to think and talk about your needs, desires, rules, wishes, and expectations—independent of your ex-spouse.

You are divorced, which means you need to see yourself as a separate person. It is time to begin reacquainting yourself with you. Who are you now as a single person? What do you really believe? What is important to you? How do you want to raise your children? What values do you want to pass on? What are your boundaries? What are your expectations?

This type of self-analysis and redefinition is important in separating yourself from your ex-spouse. This separation can help you be clear with your children about who you are as a parent. It can also help you be less reactive to the way the other parent raises your children.

Grant and Susan returned to separate religions after their divorce. Susan started taking their daughter to a Catholic church. Every other Sunday, Grant took their daughter to his Unitarian church. Each understood that the other parent was returning to religious roots and passing on what was important to him or her. Each parent was reclaiming separate identities. The parents feared that they could be doing the wrong thing, but they weren't. By staying true to personal values, they imparted the right message to their child, who grew up with a broad view of religion and deep spiritual connections.

3. Develop and use a support group to clarify the issues and a plan of action.

By adhering to the No-Load Divorce process, you have established relationships with a counselor or clergy to help you navigate the emotional riptides of divorce. These feelings don't end when the divorce is final. New emotions and stresses come into play. Continue to rely on your emotional support network. This may include divorce support groups and/or regular counseling sessions starting when you are living separately from your ex-spouse. The counselor who helped you before and during your divorce has a history with you. This counselor, who understands your issues and knows a lot about you, may be helpful as you go forward.

However, sometimes your emotional needs change after the divorce. Your focus may switch from dealing with your ex-spouse to dealing with your children—and your new self. The good news is some counselors are trained specifically in single-parent—and even stepparent—issues. Support groups abound, such as divorce support groups, single-parent support groups, and job support groups. Local places of worship and social service groups can provide you with lists.

If you start asking for help, you'll be surprised at the resources available as you move into your new life. For example, you can take community education classes on cooking, automobile maintenance, and a variety of recreational activities, to name a few. The more you develop an adult network of support, the less you will rely on your children for emotional support. This means the children won't feel caught in the middle—or responsible for your well-being (which they are not).

4. When your children ask about your ex-spouse, speak in neutral terms.

We recommend that you avoid discussing your ex-spouse in front of your children. But what if the children bring up the other parent? How do you respond? The answer is to do so in neutral terms. You want to create an environment where the children feel safe to talk about what disturbs them at the other house. You can monitor this kind of communication for danger signs, such as child abuse or neglect.

Keep in mind that the minute you make a judgment, the flow of information will stop. Suppose little Johnny says to Mom, "Dad lets us eat ice cream before dinner." The wrong response is, "I'm going to talk with your Dad about that because it's not healthy and I forbid it." Well, you can forget about Johnny ever telling you another thing about his life at Dad's house. Besides, you don't get to make the rules at Dad's house, nor does he at yours. Examples of a safer response that keeps open the lines of communication are:

- ▸ "What flavor do you like?"
- ▸ "Maybe we can go out for ice cream more often, too, but I like to do that after dinner."

In your response, don't even hint at a judgment. Don't say with a snotty attitude, "I guess Dad and I just have different rules." That is not neutral, and your children will detect it.

5. Use your divorce mediator to discuss major issues.

You may want to discuss important issues with your ex-spouse. In some cases, you may be able to discuss them on the phone or even over coffee. Drawing on the lessons you learned during your divorce, you may even resolve them on your own. In other cases, however, you'll need a process to seek resolution. Some divorced couples choose to see a counselor. Another option is to meet with your mediator. This person helped you during the divorce and is familiar with your situation, so you and your ex-spouse are probably comfortable with this person.

At what point do you call your mediator? Examples of issues or needs that may warrant a call include:

- ▶ Better ways to transfer the children during "switch times"
- ▶ Temporary change in custody due to a work assignment
- ▶ Changes in a parent's health that may affect co-parenting
- ▶ Child's chronic illness
- ▶ Child's learning disability
- ▶ Job changes that may affect alimony or child support
- ▶ Rethinking the custody schedule as the children grow older.

Keep in mind that by getting mediation or counseling help in addressing major co-parenting issues, you avoid involving your children or lawyers in your disputes.

6. When all else fails, seek a neutral third party through the courts.

Even the best of divorced parents may encounter instances when lingering anger between them prevents resolution of a co-parenting issue. You may also face a parenting issue about which you and your ex have strong and irreconcilable differences, and mediation will not resolve the problem.

An alternative to a standoff or open warfare that could confuse or emotionally scar your children is court-appointed mediation. In this case, you or your ex-spouse (or both of you) can ask the divorce court to appoint a professional to help you resolve your differences. In some states this person is called a "parenting coordinator" or a "court-appointed mediator." The person is trained in dispute resolution and often is a social worker or therapist by profession. Unlike your No-Load Divorce mediator, this person carries stronger "official" authority as a representative of the court.

Both parents go into this dispute resolution knowing two things: First, if the mediation fails, the next step is filing an order with the court, which will be costly and emotionally disruptive. Second, if the court becomes involved, the judge or representative of the judge (sometimes called a referee) will usually rely on the recommendation of the parenting coordinator you just met with. So, you might as well follow the guidance of the parenting coordinator from the start.

Parenting coordinators charge an hourly fee set by the court. The fee is usually much less than the fees you would pay for reengaging your lawyer and going back to court. The use of parenting coordinators is a reasonable recourse when you face an impasse with your ex-spouse or when one parent refuses to attempt to resolve a dispute.

›› Turning Single Parenting into a Positive Experience

Much depends on your attitude when it comes to single parenting. The challenge is to overcome the negatives—children spending less time with both parents, two sets of rules, two households, less disposable income, and the loss of the notion of "one big, happy family"—and get to the positives.

The positives, however, seem to be less obvious than the negatives, at least at first. But you will discover them. Perhaps the most obvious positive is that you can now instill your values in your children without listening to or seeing your spouse challenge or undermine you, which may have happened in your marriage. By not having to deal with your spouse's interference (at least not directly), you are free to focus your love on your children *your* way. You'll probably immediately notice that the quality of your one-on-one time with your children is better.

An important part of getting to the positives of single parenting may require a personal change. What can you do to change your attitude? The first step is to admit your loss. This seems very basic and not very positive, but your children need to know that you recognize life is different. They need to know you fully understand that the children didn't choose this new life. Don't consistently mope and cry about the divorce, but when your children give you clues that they are experiencing a moment of loss, be understanding and empathetic. If your daughter bursts out crying at bedtime and says, "I want Daddy! Now!" don't deny her feelings or feel slighted. Instead, comfort her with a response like, "I understand. I'm sorry. That must be hard."

The next step is to create a household in which your children feel secure and grow in responsibility and confidence. Read a few books on how to set up a single household. Single-parent groups meet regularly to share ideas and offer support. We also offer these suggestions:

Remember that you are the parent and your children are the children.

Many single parents rely too much on their children to help them parent. They ask the child to be a confidant or to handle adult responsibilities within the household. Don't do this to your children. Hang on to your role as parent. Set your rules and enforce them. Run the household. Children want this structure. They also want a say, but having a say is different than having equal freedom and responsibility. For example, you may decide you want your children to do chores. Assign chores but only after you involve the children in the chores discussions.

Create your own special memories.

Pam remembers growing up with her mother in a small home without a washer and dryer. Every Saturday they piled the laundry onto a red wagon and pulled it two blocks to the Laundromat. "We'd sit and watch the clothes tumble in the dryer and read silly magazines together," Pam recalls. "I suppose some kids would have wanted to be doing other things on a Saturday, but I would look forward to it. Over the years I found this to be a memory I'll cherish forever."

This story illustrates that divorce and single parenting can create opportunities you never imagined—opportunities for memories that are as important as any a child could get from a no-divorce household. Keep your eye out for your own opportunities. Pam recalled also that her dad was the only male Brownie troop leader in her town, and she brags about that. "It gave me the courage to do whatever I wanted, regardless of conventions," she says.

Aim for stability.

You have heard our pitch for stability throughout this chapter, but it is so important to children of divorce, especially as you attempt to make a positive experience out of single parenting. Try to reward your children—and yourself—with as much stability as you can in the years ahead. You can't do anything about the divorce now. It is over. However, the turmoil is probably lingering, so give your children stability wherever you can. Don't change their rooms any more than necessary, move houses just to move, parade your dates in front of them, or make promises you can't keep. Do:

- ▸ Schedule a special one-on-one time with each child once a week
- ▸ Clean the house together the same time each week
- ▸ Create special family celebrations or holidays that repeat each year
- ▸ Eat dinner at the same time each night
- ▸ Take regular vacations, including trips to a special place that you visit repeatedly.

Model courage.

Your children know this divorce is tough on you. They are watching to see how you handle this. From you, they will learn how to handle changes and stresses in their lives, now and as adults. Use this time to model the behaviors you want your children to learn and use. You can react to the divorce with anger and fear, but know that your children will take their cues from you; they will probably react the same way under stress, now and as adults.

Show courage. Look for ways to build your support network, ask for help, learn new things, and make every attempt to put a positive spin on life. You know the saying: "If given lemons, make lemonade." So make some lemonade, and in the process show your children how to do it as well. You can do this!

CHAPTER 10

The Gifts of a No-Load Divorce

You know those blessed moments when the kids are in bed and time is all yours? It can be early in the morning or later in the evening. You may have been tired not too long before, but now you are awake and full of energy—because this is finally *your* time. That is what this concluding chapter is about, your time and your future.

We focus on the new you, apart from your ex-spouse and your children. You probably have oodles of questions about the future of this new you, but the one question you have to start with is simple: How do you begin living your new life?

To answer this question, let's start by going back to the day of your divorce and the days immediately afterward.

›› Expect to Be in Shock

Many people say that what you feel when the divorce is final differs from what you expect to feel.

"I remember the day, the hour, and the minute," says our friend Rudy. "My lawyer and I walked out of the courtroom, and I felt dizzy and confused. I think I was elated. I felt like a huge weight was lifted off my shoulders. That part I expected. But it also seemed surreal. I was no longer a husband. I no longer had a wife. I was a single person. I felt like I was falling backward in time. Elation quickly gave way to fear, and the fear was BIG. All I could do was ask myself the same question, over and over: Now what?"

This reaction of shock is startling but typical. U.S. journalist Helen Rowland once wrote the following: "Love, the quest; marriage, the conquest; divorce, the inquest." Of course you are in shock because you have survived the inquest, and the world you knew is now dramatically different. Your identity has been changed by the stroke of the judge's pen. The good news here is that the shock probably won't last long. "Usually, closure on a divorce doesn't take a great deal of time," says Minneapolis divorce attorney Carole M. Megarry. "These people have been very unhappy for a long time and are ready to move on. While they were in the middle of the divorce, it was like ripping a scab off a wound each time an issue needed to be resolved. Now that the divorce is final, it feels good to stop ripping the scab and let healing begin. Psychologists say that healing from a divorce does not start until the decree is entered."

What will also help you shake off the shock and start healing is this: You face a long list of things you have to do (some you may already have done), including the following (see next page):

You may feel buried under your long list of to-dos and definitely not free to launch into your new life. If so, remember the donkey fable, which goes like this:

One day a farmer's donkey fell into an abandoned well. The farmer and his neighbors tried every way they could think of to pull the donkey out. Each method failed, and so the farmer decided to bury the donkey. The group began shoveling, and the donkey began wailing horribly. After many more shovelfuls, the wailing stopped. The farmer peered down the well and was astonished. The donkey was refusing to be buried! The animal would shake off the descending dirt and then stand on it. The farmer ordered the shoveling to continue, and slowly but surely the donkey rose from the depths of the well. Pretty soon, the donkey stepped up over the edge of the well and trotted off.

And the moral? Don't be buried by all the details of setting up a post-divorce life. Instead, think of the to-dos as small steps toward creating your new you.

›› Accepting the Divorce as Final

Some people can get rather mulish (pardon the pun) about not ending their marriage—even after the divorce is final. They cling to their old life, often by continuing with the same bitter feuds that plagued their marriage and divorce. They fail to come to closure and therefore fail to take a major step in building a new life. We don't want you to make this mistake, so we have come up with the following five ways for you to accept the divorce as final.

›› 20 (OF 1,000) TO-DOS FOR DIVORCED PARENTS

1. Arrange for a separate residence

2. Learn different routes to work, grocery stores, gas stations, video stores, libraries, etc.

3. Make arrangements to see your children

4. Notify their school of the divorce and make arrangements to receive the same notices about events, grades, and conferences that your spouse does

5. Establish your own credit

6. Separate assets and property ownership according to the divorce agreement

7. Fill out change-of-address forms

8. Get a new phone number and Internet connection

9. Tell your family and friends that the divorce is final

10. Decide who will remain your friends and who will be your ex-spouse's friends

11. Decide whether you will attend the same place of worship as your ex-spouse

12. Buy essentials that went to your spouse, like silverware, towels, sheets, or a television set

13. Figure out how to spend recreational time and Saturday evenings

14. Find a grief support group

15. Find professional help in fighting depression and anger

16. Set up bedrooms, and buy clothes for your children

17. Learn new skills such as cooking, carpentry, car maintenance, and laundry

18. Reestablish a relationship with your ex in-laws

19. Pay legal bills

20. Decide what to do with your wedding ring.

Get "unmarried."

Immediately after the divorce, you may be tempted to act like you are still married. Some ex-spouses talk to each other daily, keep the other's picture close at hand, and stop by each other's house to help with chores. However, to feel divorced and begin to experience closure, you need to limit contact with each other. You need to begin living separate lives.

You may even find that you have an odd interest in getting back together with your ex. It happens. Our advice is lie down and let the feeling pass. Robyn says, "Every time I got to thinking I should have tried harder and that maybe we could make this work, I'd remember Tom's violent behavior and know it was the right decision to move on."

Your efforts now are not to patch up the past but to find your future—separate from your ex.

Grieve the loss.

Divorce is a loss, and a loss requires grieving. Some divorced people don't grieve well. They skip it, basically, or at least they try to. They say they've washed their hands of the whole thing because they hate the ex-spouse. At the other extreme, some divorced people don't really close the book on the marriage. They keep it alive in their mind by pining away in self-recrimination, wondering if they'd still be married if they had just handled some things better.

As painful as grieving is, you have to do it. "A divorce is like someone died—but there is no funeral," says Robyn. Often there is no ceremony or process to help you feel the anger, confusion, despair, helplessness, and loss, and, just as importantly, to help you get to the healing side—to the excitement, confidence-building, and recovery. Therefore, we recommend doing something symbolic that recognizes the end. Perhaps write a letter saying goodbye to the ex-spouse (don't mail it), keep a journal to mark your progress, or invite friends to a dinner and make a toast to new beginnings.

Prepare a concise explanation.

Placement services tell job seekers to prepare a concise explanation about why they are not working for their past employer and what they have to offer a new employer. The explanation demonstrates the job seeker's intent to leave the past behind and move forward without hesitation. We advise newly divorced people to prepare a similar explanation, without blaming the ex-spouse.

It may help you to talk with others about a difficult part of your life, and it serves a greater purpose of helping you come to terms with the divorce. Psychologists say it may also help to write about why you got married, what the difficulties in the marriage were, what role each of you played in the conflicts, and what you want from your new life. This kind of explanation will help you accept that the marriage is over.

Share the blame.

Make no mistake about it: You both had a part in the divorce. If you focus only on your ex-spouse's errors, you become a victim and stay linked to your ex-spouse through feelings of bitterness. However, if you focus on your own mistakes, you open the door to examining ways you might change your behavior in new relationships. It will free you to grow and avoid the mistakes of the past.

A second part of this step is to forgive your ex-spouse. This may not be easy, and it will take time. But by forgiving your ex-spouse, psychologists say, you are really forgiving yourself for your mistakes in the marriage. Forgiveness will free you to move on with life. Writer Roberto Assagioli once said, "Without forgiveness life is governed by . . . an endless cycle of resentment and retaliation."

Look ahead.

Looking ahead after a divorce can be a grieving-and-waiting situation. You may feel the need to grieve the loss and accept the divorce before discovering a whole new world of opportunity waiting. You may find that embracing new opportunities will help you accept your divorce. You might try an evening class in cooking, for example, or volunteer in an organization that interests you. By filling your life with new things, you begin to detach from old ways and move forward.

›› Continuing to Put Your Financial Life in Order

Before her divorce, Robyn did a post-divorce budget to help her see clearly what she could do for herself and what she needed from her soon-to-be ex-spouse. The support she received in the divorce settlement was exactly what she budgeted, and she proceeded to live a new life within her means.

"Life after divorce is not scary when you know you can do it," Robyn says. "I went at it not clinging to him financially, not being in a place of fear. I was able to relax and allow things to work out. And I was able to let go of the marriage better. Had I been fearful and needy financially, I may have changed my mind about the divorce. But I wasn't, and therefore I was able to say to myself, 'I did the best I could'—and then move on."

Now that you are divorced, you should be like Robyn, keen about taking care of your finances. Now is the time to meet with your financial adviser, who will continue to guide you as you put your financial house in order after the divorce. Your adviser will help you:

- ▸ Retitle assets assigned to you by your divorce stipulation and decree. Retitling involves naming the owner of the assets and the beneficiary of the assets should you die.

- ▸ Adjust beneficiary designations (you may want beneficiaries to be a trust).

- ▸ Determine which QDRO settlements are best for you (settlements from qualified plans). One option is to roll 100 percent of the money to a self-directed IRA. Another option is to take a distribution of part or all of the plan without IRS penalties (however, significant taxes will be paid).

- ▸ Assess your personal insurance needs. These includes life insurance, disability insurance, homeowner's/liability insurance, auto insurance, and long-term care coverage.

- ▸ Secure insurance on your ex-spouse to cover child support and alimony payments in the event of your ex-spouse's death, if applicable. This should have been done prior to agreement on the settlement.

- ▸ Reexamine investment objectives and current allocations and do an overall review of goals (college funding, retirement, purchasing a second home, etc.).

Your financial adviser will help you decide whether it is in your best interest to set up a trust. This decision depends on many factors, such as the ages of your children and how and when you want the assets distributed. A trust allows for your assets to be applied to your children as you wish. In some cases, if you do not have a trust, control of your assets could revert to your ex-spouse. If you need a trust, your financial adviser can refer you to a lawyer who specializes in estate planning.

As a result of your financial negotiations and divorce settlement, you now know your monthly income. If you were the principal wage earner in the marriage, your new income may be reduced by child support and alimony payments. If you were not working, your new income may consist of child support and/or alimony payments. In either case, you likely face many new expenses that you didn't have before the divorce. To cope with this new financial life day to day, you need to establish a new monthly budget.

A budget is a plan that covers your income and expenses. Obviously, you want to structure your budget so that your expenses do not exceed your income. Then you must stick to the budget. The alternative is to incur debt, usually credit card debt. We strongly discourage this. You would be creating a hole out of which it is difficult to climb. Credit card companies lure you with attractive "introductory" interest rates. Many people find it a challenge just to make the minimum payment, making it impossible to eliminate the debt.

The best way to avoid debt is to use your monthly budget to control spending and keep expenses less than your income. To create a budget, first list your average monthly expenses. (If some bills are paid once a year, divide them by 12.) Here's a sample list of expenses (see next page):

Many people who go through this exercise find that their expenses exceed their income. If you are in this situation, look for ways to cut your expenses. Start with trimming your discretionary and entertainment expenses.

Review your consumer debt. Pay it off quickly to avoid large interest charges. If you are not able to do this, you may be able to restructure the debt through a debt-consolidation loan or home refinancing.

Those are the basics of budgets. Work with your financial adviser to go beyond the basics in covering long-term financial goals, such as saving for your children's post-high-school education or your retirement.

›› TYPICAL MONTHLY EXPENSES

Mortgage or rent (if a mortgage, include your principal and interest payment)

Utilities (electricity, phone, gas, oil, water, sewage)

Home upkeep (repair, painting, etc.)

Food (groceries)

Health care (prescriptions, office visits, medications)

Insurance (car, home, disability, health, dental, life, etc.)

Auto payment and upkeep (gas, oil changes, repair, license costs)

Taxes (property, income)

Entertainment (movies, restaurants, travel)

Credit card and other debt payments

Discretionary (hairdresser, golf green fees, club memberships, vacations, home decorating, computers, and Internet access fees)

›› TYPICAL MONTHLY INCOME

Wages, salary, business profit, tips

Alimony (add this if you are receiving alimony; subtract it if you are paying alimony)

Child support (add this if you are receiving child support; subtract it if you are paying child support)

Interest income (in most cases this should not be considered income unless you are already retired)

Investment income

Three quick tips about budgets:

1. Keep on eye on discretionary spending. People often discover they can get by just fine by cutting their discretionary spending. They tell us they were not aware of how much money they were spending on "nice-to-haves" rather than "need-to-haves."

Keeping a list of every purchase will open your eyes to spending habits you weren't aware of.

2. Put your children on a budget as well. Let them know how much they can spend on clothes, entertainment, and the like. Encourage them to make their own choices and to face the consequences of spending their allowance too soon. Encourage your children to get a part-time job when they demonstrate they can be responsible.

3. You also can seek a job or career if you haven't already done so. A job not only can add to your income but may give you a sense of purpose that will help you get through your adjustment to the divorce.

›› The Gifts of No-Load Divorce

We are winding down here, so it's time for review. We want to remind you of special gifts you have given yourself by completing the No-Load Divorce. Because you had the courage, maturity, and civility to follow the process in this book, you have acquired skills and benefits that will help you in your new life.

Empowerment.

You chose not to be a victim, driven by anger and revenge. Instead, you faced your fears, accepted your part of the failed marriage, and put aside your bitterness to work with your ex-spouse to achieve a fair settlement. You rolled up your sleeves, learned to ask for what you want, and negotiated to reach consensus.

Self-respect.

You have survived the divorce with the respect of your ex-spouse, your children, and yourself. You have demonstrated restraint, a respect for boundaries, and a willingness to seek resolution and compromise. You have treated all parties with dignity, and that dignity now comes back to you.

›› HARD LESSONS BUT NOT A HARD HEART

Peggy is our No-Load Divorce Poster Person. She is a model for how to go through a divorce, come to closure, and move on with a new life.

Peggy and Paul met and married in college. They raised two children, had careers, and did volunteer work. This made for what appeared to be a good marriage, but it wasn't. Their active, full lives served as a "good buffer for us, allowing us to not deal with stuff," says Peggy.

Much of the "stuff" centered on Peggy's low self-esteem and Paul's depression. She didn't want to make waves or create conflict, and he was too down to talk about issues anyway. So over the course of their 25-year marriage, they drifted apart. Finally, after a trip to France that was a flop, Peggy moved out and told a shocked and crushed Paul that she wanted a divorce. "I couldn't see a way for me to remain me and still remain married," she recalls.

These were hard times, but to their credit, Peggy and Paul kept their wits about them as they started divorce proceedings. They avoided the lure of letting lawyers do all the work. They did their best to divide assets on their own. Their children were adults, so custody was not an issue. But they agreed that each of them would write separate letters to their children, explaining the divorce.

Then Peggy and Paul went to a mediator. "We looked at mediation as an economic issue," says Peggy. "We had done as much as we could, and we saw mediation as a cheaper route than going to a lawyer right away."

They did four sessions of mediation at $175 per session. "Even mediation was costly to us," says Peggy. "The major reason we felt that way was we had already done most of the dividing of assets, so we wondered why should we spend time and money hashing this out again in front of a mediator."

The mediator recommended that Peggy and Paul see a counselor to help them arrive at closure. They did four sessions with this counselor, at $125 per session.

Hard Lessons But Not a Hard Heart continued on next page

Hard Lessons But Not a Hard Heart continued from previous page

The largest cost, not surprisingly, was their lawyers' fees. Peggy and Paul each paid $800 for separate lawyers. "We knew the bill could be big unless we kept the lawyers in check," says Peggy. "Both lawyers were rational and efficient. They only went back and forth once. We had some concerns that they would try to stir things up, but we didn't let that happen."

All told, then, Peggy and Paul spent $1,350 each for their divorce, which became final in 1995. It was truly a No-Load Divorce before such a thing existed.

Paul remarried, and Peggy is in a loving relationship. They have moved on with their lives, coming to closure about their marriage. This is not to say, however, that Peggy does not have feelings about Paul and the divorce. She does and always will, in part because of the respectful way she went through the divorce. She did not become consumed with everlasting bitterness. Instead, she has room in her heart to experience a full range of emotions appropriate to the loss.

"Paul and I were together at a confirmation—we were sponsors—and I felt so guilty to see Paul so happy," says Peggy. "That is, his new wife was so sweet and accepting of him, and just a few years before it was a painful divorce I had visited upon him. But maybe the divorce was the catalyst Paul needed to deal with his depression."

In tears, Peggy explains that she probably will always feel some guilt and pain about the divorce. "I saw Paul as vulnerable because of the depression, and here I was heaping one more difficulty on him," she says. "I came from a fairly traditional, conservative family that believed once you said those marriage vows, you did not turn your back on the other person. I'm still not comfortable with it."

So is this closure? Yes, we like to view this as the best kind of closure. Closure does not mean developing amnesia and denial about the divorce. It does not mean becoming cold and hard-hearted, and therefore hampered as you try to enter new relationships. It does not mean a "line in the sand" cutting off the old life from the new.

Hard Lessons But Not a Hard Heart continued on next page

Hard Lessons But Not a Hard Heart continued from previous page

Closure means honest endings. Peggy's tears and honesty show that she cares, always has and always will. Divorce, thankfully, did not rob her of a vital part of her humanity—her capacity to care and tell the truth.

With closure, you will look back from time to time, with regrets and even gratitude. But these moments don't last long because your eyes are increasingly more interested in what lies ahead. You move on knowing that the hard lessons of divorce have not made *you* hard.

"It is interesting to see the number of ways to get to where you need to be," says Peggy. "I'm a better partner now, compared with when I was married to Paul because I am willing to speak up for myself. My prescription for young women is certainly not to go through a divorce in order to learn what you need in life. But my thinking is, if I have to be on this road, I guess I might as well learn along the way."

Financial responsibility.

If you have learned nothing else in this book, you have learned not to be like our friend Mike. Mike and his soon-to-be ex-wife split their assets themselves and agreed on the division. Then they made the classic mistake of hiring lawyers and giving them the keys to the kingdom. That move cost them $20,000 in legal fees. And the kicker is, when the final settlement was reached, it was within $500 of the figure Mike and his ex agreed on originally. That means they spent $20,000 so one of them could gain $500.

You have learned not to make Mike's kind of mistake. In addition, the No-Load Divorce process has helped you get a better fix on your financial situation, investments, insurance, and budgeting. You and your ex-spouse have done your best to reach a financial settlement that will enable each of you to become more economically self-sufficient, while giving your children the best life you can.

Networking.

You have developed a No-Load Divorce team, including a financial adviser, a counselor or therapist, clergy, support groups, and friends. This team will be available to you as you face the challenges of adapting to your single life. If you were alone or isolated before following this process, you are no longer.

Communications.

Unlike the majority of divorced couples, you and your ex-spouse worked together and now have a template for dealing with co-parenting issues going forward. Because you haven't intentionally tried to hurt each other, you are able to cooperate and compromise. You have built up respect for each other that will make you both better parents, and better people.

Rediscovery.

You have shown to yourself and to your children strengths and adaptability that you never thought you had. You have tried new things, even fun things, and have opened yourself up to all the surprises, joys, and sorrows of single parenting and single life. In this way, you have discovered new characteristics about yourself—or unearthed old ones—that you can take with pride into your new life.

Money.

In addition to the emotional gifts that you receive, you and your family will have added financial resources that would have gone to lawyers. This money now can be spent on things like college funding, vacations, paying off consumer debt, purchasing a new home, and beginning your new life.

Closure.

As hard as the transition to a new life is, the switch will be easier because you have done the difficult emotional work of a No-Load Divorce. You have examined your marriage, made certain in your heart and mind that it needed to end, tied up scores of emotional loose ends, experienced success in negotiating with your ex-spouse, and finished the divorce. All of these victories in closure will help you move forward.

›› How Can I Avoid Making the Same Mistake Twice?

Clients who have been divorced frequently ask, "How can I be sure I don't repeat the same mistake as I look for another relationship?" They may laugh at the man in the joke below, who seems like the type who has a blind spot about fidelity and is doomed to make the same mistake throughout his life. While they may laugh, they may also fear discovering their own blind spots in picking their next partner.

> WOMAN: What would you do if I died? Would you get married again?
>
> MAN: Definitely not!
>
> WOMAN: Why not—don't you like being married?
>
> MAN: Of course I do.
>
> WOMAN: Then why wouldn't you remarry?
>
> MAN: Okay, I'd get married again.
>
> WOMAN: You would? *(with a hurtful look on her face)*
>
> MAN: *(makes audible groan)*
>
> WOMAN: Would you sleep with her in our bed?
>
> MAN: Where else would we sleep?
>
> WOMAN: Would you replace my pictures with hers?
>
> MAN: That would seem like the proper thing to do.
>
> WOMAN: Would she use my golf clubs?
>
> MAN: No, she's left-handed.
>
> WOMAN: *(silence)*
>
> MAN: Whoops.

"You *will* make the same mistake again—unless you develop more awareness around your choice of partners," says Jean Naymark, who for

24 years has been a licensed clinical social worker and licensed marriage and family therapist in the Minneapolis–St. Paul area. "Otherwise, even if your new mate appears different, over time he or she will turn into a carbon copy of your first spouse."

Naymark gives this example. "I have a client who came to me after his third marriage. Every one of his wives was an alcoholic. He doesn't drink. What brought him into counseling was he was sure his third wife was different from all the rest. She seemed less introverted and more self-sufficient. After he married her, he saw she too was an alcoholic!

"This man likes to be in control of the women he marries. He likes to be a caretaker because it makes him feel important. So, he's a walking magnet for alcoholics, and this isn't going to change until *he* changes."

Naymark says that as you move on after a divorce, you must focus on your own relationship issues, not your ex-spouse's. "I can't tell you how many couples come in here and stay in counseling until they get divorced. Then they end counseling, thinking the problem is their ex-spouse. Five years later, they call me and say they want to get divorced from their second wife or husband. They're amazed that they are experiencing the same problems all over again. I tell them, 'The problem isn't your partner—it's you.' "

Changing you can take time. Naymark says that after a long marriage, it may take three to five years of counseling and healing before you're ready to make a better choice regarding your next mate. So be patient.

"My experience is that people who really want to know themselves better will have the most success in future marriages," Naymark says.

›› Final Thoughts From the Editors

When Bill spent $25,000 on a nasty divorce, he swore that there has to be a better way.

After the divorce was over, there continued to be constant conflict between Bill and his ex-wife—and a few times with her second husband. He spent another $20,000 on an attempted change in custody. Bill has dealt with hassles about changing schools and vacations with the kids. Bill knows that his children love him, but he also knows that because of limited custody time, it's more difficult to maintain as strong a connection as he would have when living with them. He thinks about his children all the time, even when they are not with him. The ramifications of this divorce go on and on.

The divorce has changed Bill. He admits he used to drive himself and others too hard. He's mellowed a bit, now calling himself an "amiable driver." He enjoys the freedom of the single life, the chance for a fresh start. When he is with his children, they have his full attention because he is not distracted by a conflicted relationship with his ex-spouse. Since his divorce, business has improved because he doesn't have everyday domestic distractions weighing on him.

Bill admits that he is slow to trust the women he dates. It is not the women, necessarily. It's the scars he carries from the divorce. He's not sure he wants to go through with marriage again, and yet he is not sure he wants to remain single. He hopes that time—and some divine intervention, perhaps—will heal his wounds.

Bill is still upset about the process he went through to get a divorce. He has come to understand that he is upset with himself as well for not knowing what to do during a divorce and for not taking the time to find out. "Part of this is my fault, for not knowing what I should have known," he says. "But who has that time to find out when your head is spinning?" So he relied on the legal system and paid heavily—and is still paying heavily—for it.

In the meantime, he has devoted a good deal of energy to develop a better way for couples to get divorced, if divorce is their only option.

As a result of that effort, Bill collaborated with Steve to write this book. Together, they found there was a better way. They want you to learn from the examples of Bill and the dozens of other people you have read about in these pages. They want you to be in the know so that you can be respectful and savvy during the divorce. When the divorce is finished, they want you to feel upbeat about your future.

Bill and Steve sincerely hope that their book has helped you and will help you in the years ahead. Drop them a line on their Web site (www.noloaddivorce.com), and let them know. Please pass on this book to friends contemplating divorce so that they too may escape the typical but unnecessary financial and emotional divorce loads. As difficult as a divorce is, there is a better way to go through the process—the No-Load Divorce way.

Sample Divorce Settlements

The following settlements are based on a composite of actual cases. We altered names and personal situations to protect the privacy of the parties. Any resemblance to real persons is coincidental and unintended. *These three cases were settled in Michigan and based on guidelines established by the State of Michigan.*

›› Mary and John Hansen

Situation

Married 20 years. Mary earns $60,000; John earns $80,000 a year. The couple has three sons, ages 10, 15, and 17.

Divorce Custody Arrangement

The couple is awarded joint legal custody, with alternating weeks beginning Friday evenings. The parties agree to "use their best efforts to work together to ensure consistency and agreement in matters affecting the upbringing of the children." The couple alternates holidays and special events each year. The children are with their mother on her birthday and Mother's Day. The children are with their father on his birthday and Father's Day. "Neither party shall exercise overnight parenting time in the presence of an unrelated, non-family member of the opposite sex." The parents agree not to change the domicile of the children to more than 100 miles from their present home. (The father will retain possession of the family dogs.)

Divorce Financial Settlement

- Neither parent receives spousal support.

- The father pays the mother $30 per child per month in accordance with county guidelines (based on the disparity between their incomes) until that child reaches age 18.

- Since both parents receive health care coverage at work, they will decide which parent covers the children and split any additional cost in proportion to their incomes.

- Parents will pay the children's uninsured health costs in proportion to their incomes.

- Parents will sell the current home and split the net profits.

- Mary and John will keep their individual cars and assume financial responsibility for that car.

- Each person will retain assets owned entering the marriage or given them by relatives.

- All joint property will be split evenly.

- The couple will establish a joint account to pay off joint debt.

- Each party will receive half interest in the other's retirement accounts, but only to amounts created during the marriage.

- Going forward, each person is responsible for his or her own debt.

- Each party is responsible for his or her own attorney fees.

›› Jane and Bill Smith

Situation

Married 20 years. Both are 48 years old. Jane has a high school education. Bill has a college graduate degree. Jane is a homemaker with no outside income. Bill earns $100,000 a year. They have two sons, ages 15 and 17.

Divorce Custody Arrangement

Jane and Bill agree to joint legal custody of the children. Jane has full legal custody. Bill has parenting time on alternate weekends and one evening a week, as well as two weeks of vacation with the children each year. Parents alternate major holidays .

Divorce Financial Settlement

- Because of the disparity in the parents' income and education, Bill is ordered to pay Jane $1,628 in spousal support per month for 10 years. This support will end if and when Jane remarries. The payments are taxable to Jane and are deductible for Bill.

- According to county child support guidelines, Bill will pay $354 a week until his first son reaches age 18, and then $230 a week until his second son reaches that age.

- Bill will take out a term life insurance policy to cover his total spousal support and child support obligations, with Jane as the beneficiary.

- Bill will pay for health insurance and 90 percent of health care costs for the children.

- Bill will transfer ownership of both the family home and the family lake cottage to Jane, who then becomes responsible for all upkeep costs and mortgage payments.

- Jane will be awarded half interest in Bill's retirement accounts, but only applied to amounts created during the marriage.

- Each person will retain assets they owned entering the marriage or given them by relatives.

- The couple has two cars. Each is awarded one of the cars and assumes all costs for that car.

- All investment assets are split 50-50, as well as all other property and furnishings.

- Bill will pay balances on all joint credit cards and close the accounts.

- Mary and Bill each will have one child exemption for income tax purposes. When the older child becomes independent, they will alternate the remaining exemption each year.

- Each party is responsible for his or her own attorney fees.

›› Kim and Dave Williams

Situation

Married five years. Kim earns $25,000 a year. Dave earns $80,000 a year. Their one child attends daycare that costs $125 a week. The couple lives in a rented townhome.

Divorce Custody Arrangement

Kim and Dave have joint legal custody of their daughter, Jennifer, who is 3 years old. Kim is awarded sole physical custody. Dave has parenting time on alternate weekends and one evening on the weeks when he does not see his daughter that weekend, He also has two weeks of vacation with his daughter each year. Parents alternate major holidays.

Divorce Financial Settlement

- Kim is awarded $175 a week for 6 months to make the transition to being self-supporting. Other than this "rehabilitative alimony," no alimony or spousal support is ordered.

- Because of the disparity in their incomes, Dave is ordered to pay Kim $266 per week in child support until Jennifer reaches age 19 1/2 (18 if she does not continue her education until age 19 1/2). The amount follows county guidelines based on the disparity of their incomes.

- Kim will remain with Jennifer in the current townhome and will assume rental costs. Dave will be responsible for his housing costs.

- Dave will pay for health insurance for Jennifer and 75 percent of health care costs for her. Kim will pay 25 percent.

- All investment assets are split 50-50, as well as all other property and furnishings.

- Kim will be awarded half interest in Dave's retirement accounts, applied to amounts created during the marriage.

- Dave will pay balances on all joint credit cards and close the accounts.

- Kim is awarded the annual income tax exemption of her daughter.

- All insurance owned by either Kim or Dave is to be owned free and clear of the other person, without obligation to name the other person as beneficiary.

- Each person will retain assets owned entering the marriage or given them by their relatives.

- Each party is responsible for his or her own attorney fees.

- Dave will carry term life insurance to cover future child support payments. The beneficiary will be Jennifer or a trust for her benefit.

Authors

BILL KUMM graduated from Central Michigan University in 1987 with a major in finance. He currently holds a Series 7, 63, 65, Life and Health Variable Contracts License. Bill is also a Registered Representative and Investment Advisor Associate.

Since 1993 Bill has been lecturing and leading education groups on the subject of personal finance. In 1995 Bill co-founded Financial Independence, Inc., a firm that specializes in financial and retirement planning, located in Bloomfield Hills, Michigan.

Bill went through a divorce in 1996 and 1997. Through this experience, including a difficult custody battle, Bill learned some very expensive financial and emotional lessons. These lessons inspired Bill and his partner, Steve Case, to write this book. Bill's hope is that this book will help both adults and children avoid suffering caused by a contentious divorce.

STEVE CASE graduated from Cornell University with a degree in business administration and applied economics in 1987. He is a Certified Financial Planner and a Registered Representative and Investment Advisor Associate.

Steve has been a keynote speaker and educator on the subject of personal finance. He is one of the founders and senior partners of Financial Independence, Inc.

Steve has counseled many clients through the financial aspects of divorce and has seen the damages that the process can bring. He was inspired to co-write this book after observing his partner Bill Kumm's divorce. Steve hopes this book will help couples avoid the often needless suffering of a contentious divorce.